Carmel Austin & Friends Present:

The Artist
Haven

Fourteen Empowered Stories to Overcome Obstacles and Embrace Creative Expression

Editing & format/layout by: Chelsia McCoy/*Your Writing Table* (www.yourwritingtable.com)
Bookcover Design: Angela Günther, original artwork.

As Carmel Austin, the visionary and lead author is Australian, the book will adhere to the conventions of Australian English in each of the chapters.
All artwork, poetry & songs are original works as created by the authors.
Any works not created by the authors will have references provided.

Carmel's Garden

Carmel Austin Publishing
Unified Voices

Carmel Austin & Friends Present...

'Creative expressions of the Heart'... As the visionary of our book, I would like to honour Angela's artwork. This beautiful cover expresses The Artist Haven so well! Resting in a safe haven gives creatives a place to restore their souls. In this book, we share stories from our hearts and unite together as friends, telling of our experiences with courage and passion.
~Carmel Austin

TABLE OF CONTENTS

PREFACE

The title, *Artist Haven,* was inspired by a deep desire to see others shine in their talents with no boundaries or hidden agendas where they can create and thrive by setting people up with self-confidence, and the ability to express from their authentic selves with no limits. By creating this space for the intuitive mind to play and not be labeled as the wounded, lost, talented misfits that the world can be referred to. *The Artist Haven* is a place to thrive in your gifts without having your wings clipped, guiding the next generation into their destiny by expressing their artistic hopes and dreams.

As the visionary of this book, it was important for me to create a space that gives the writer freedom to thrive while giving the reader a place to explore and grow in their talents and artistic gifts. I desire to create platforms to help others see beauty in creativity by seeing their reflection clearly as if they are looking into a crystal clear stream.

As a Wholeness Coach, I have observed that many women can find themselves lost when their children have grown or when their nest is empty and they don't know how to fill it up. For this reason, they have hidden dreams inside themselves that need a gentle nudge to flourish. For men, this transition may be a little easier. Often men have been the primary financial providers and have spent many years working away from the home. Men can find when they move into retirement they have more time to explore their creativity.

This depends on how the family structure is placed as each home is different and unique. This is the reason why so many people have hidden talents and dreams that need to be nurtured in a *Safe HAVEN*.

As I started to give wings to this idea, people came out of the woodwork telling me they had a dream to write and share their story and they just needed a *Safe HAVEN* to be guided to do so.

In that account, I present to you this collaboration, a collection of stories that will delight your heart and touch the deepest parts of your soul. *The Artist Haven* unfolds into a beautiful tapestry of hope and faith. Each author bares their soul to share a simple but true story of hardship and courage that will uplift and inspire you to move forward in your creative uniqueness.

This perspective links our hearts and minds together as living souls who recognize that our broken pieces in life create beauty and love. I have found a common thread with each author, even though they have a unique voice and story to share. Their stories are intertwined with my personal anecdote bringing together a beautiful masterpiece of life and relationship that will live on beyond the written word.

Carmel Austin

> *"When all else fails, allow love to*
> *guide you on your path."*
> *~ Coach Carmel Austin*

Dedication

I dedicate my chapter to my soul mate, my amazing husband Wayne Austin. He is my best friend and the love of my life. We met as teenagers and he has been by my side every day since. Wayne is a true artisan who supports my dreams with his unique creativity as we create rustic frames together to complement my artwork that we proudly display in our home as well as his quirky handmade recycled wood stands. I am blessed beyond imagination to be his wife, as we partner together to live our best life.

~ Your loving wife, Carmel

Developing the Negative into a Positive!

Carmel Austin

Artist, Designer, Wholeness Life Coach,
Podcast Host & Media Expert

Shoalhaven NSW, Australia

"Art will remain the most astonishing activity of mankind born out of struggle between wisdom and madness, between dream and reality in our mind."
~ Magdalena Abakanowicz[1]

Creating Beauty from the Ashes of Life

I grew up with an inferiority complex and for many years, I allowed negativity to control my thoughts. I was more concerned about what other people thought about how I looked or what they said about me. I got caught in my mind's eye worrying about what might happen and never really allowed the positive images to develop.

Gifted with many talents, I have moved from pillar to post over my life, half developing the picture I saw to see if this was the path I wanted to walk down.

---

[1] QuoteFancy. (2023). Retrieved from:
https://quotefancy.com/quote/1610347/Magdalena-Abakanowicz-Art-will-remain-the-most-astonishing-activity-of-mankind-born-out

I remember studying photography back in the days when you had to enter the dark room behind a curtain where photos were developed and processed. Stepping into this unique room and watching the developing stages take place, the process of transforming the pictures I had taken into images that I could cherish and enjoy delighted my soul. The colour came to life from the black & white negative right before my eyes.

I use my God-given talents and express them on the canvas of life. I love to create and see a design in my mind's eye and then bring the pattern to life through a thought, an expression, or a vision.

As an artisan, I get to explore the beauty around me and recreate it with my passion and creativity as I permit myself to shine. Within my creative space, I allow myself room to blossom with the right ingredients that cultivate what is needed to develop and thrive. By giving my creative ideas room to express themselves at each step of the journey. "When I see the finished artwork, sewing piece or quilt, my photography and even over the meal I prepare with love for my family, I know my creativity has been captured."

But let me ask you, yes, you!

Have you ever dreamed of tapping into your intuitive self? Are you allowing yourself to express your creativity and flow freely?

Close your eyes. What picture develops in your mind's eye? Can you place it there and make the design come to life?

I believe we are all born with creative abilities. You may have explored this when you were young and now it's neatly packed away in a box in your cupboard. You may even think," I will get to that one day!"

Then that one day you've promised yourself may never come if you allow the cares of this world to entangle your dreams and goals. Let me encourage you to explore your creative authentic self.

Seeing all the elements come together with my designs when I create my quilts is like watching my thoughts and dreams pop. Allowing oneself to play this way brings creativity together with balance and satisfaction.

My mind's eye is always creating shapes and colours that bring my designs to life. One of my greatest loves is making children's quilts. As I visualize the pattern in my mind, I purchase the material that matches and blends to lay out the pattern on my table.

As I create for our grandbabies, they become heirlooms of treasure in my heart and family. I love expressing myself creatively. These activities are expressed in my sewing, writing, painting, drawing, cooking, and building websites.

Give me a vase with a unique shape or an empty wine bottle and a piece of fruit! And I will create something with my pencils that draws out the beauty of creativity as it comes to life with texture and style.

I encourage you to be your creative self and express the artist you are designed to be by allowing yourself to shine. Dream big, and don't let the things that have happened in your life stop you from being authentic and creative.

We can be so bogged down by what other people do and think about us. Consequently, this can cause our hearts and minds to be closed from the beauty of life and stop our creativity and strength and as a result, making our hearts become like stone.

As God's children, we are uniquely designed in our mother's womb, as children ready to be developed under the keen eye of the Creator hidden in darkness. Our life experiences are not meant to make us stumble, or to cause our hearts to become cold and hard. Even more so, our life circumstances are not meant to turn us into statues of despair. They are meant to help us grow and develop beautiful designs that give life and hope to the world around us.

Allow Yourself to Dream and Create

When we take time to allow creativity to rise it brings us a sense of wellness. For me, I enjoy walking in the bush with my dog and breathing in the scent of nature, hearing the rustling of leaves, smelling the combination of floral scents from the flowers all around, and the earthy scent given off by the trees around me. Taking in the beauty of nature ignites the creative in me!

I also love to enjoy exploring nature by jumping on the back of my hubby's motorbike as we travel up to Kiama to a lookout called, "The Blowhole." There is a section in the rock that has been carved out by water where it gushes out and up soaking all who have ventured too close causing a huge wave. It's fun admiring nature and its beauty while allowing my adventurous self to overtake me.

Living in Australia, it has been in my blood to enjoy the Aussie beaches. I delight in walking along the beach, exploring the tracks, and seeing my feet leave footprints in the sand as I look back. The sand absorbs me into the waves as they wash over my feet. Having the privilege to travel along these pristine beaches has given me great joy and appreciation for God's creation.

I like to take the time to stop and smell the native bushes, I enjoy adorning the intriguing structure of flowers and the amazing fragrance they give us. As a lover of the great outdoors, I am interested in plants, animals and nature.

I had the privilege to travel to the south coast of NSW as a young girl visiting Callala Bay at my Auntie's house. My fondest childhood memories were made there. There was a pink cockatoo who chatted with me, the large seashells on the seashore, and experiencing the wild horses and the bush honey. The beach is my happy place and brings up memories of laughing, playing, and swimming as we explore the beauty around us.

But let me ask you: Do you have memories locked inside of you? Are they alive in vivid colours, and you are daring to dream? Are you allowing these memories to come alive on canvas or in a tune?

I encourage you to explore your gifts and live from your authenticity, where you give yourself permission to shine. As you do this, you will bring beauty and colour to the world by expressing your unique God-given gifts and talents.

Take a moment to reflect... What have you dreamed of doing that delights your heart and soul?

As a creative coach, I encourage you to spend time bringing your dreams and goals to life. As a woman, I was taught to serve my husband, family, and community, but through this process, I lost parts of myself and was not shining and developing my gifts and talents. It has taken years for me to come to my true identity. For example, I dreamed for decades of being a published author.

I had to allow myself to cut through the thick dense forest in my mind's eye. Often taking a machete to it and carving away the layers of unbelief and doubt while capturing the lies that had built up over the decades to finally see my reflection as I peered into the river of my life. I see my life as a river that ebbs and flows through different streams and riverbanks that flow into different lakes.

Thus, one of the reasons I have created the *Artistic Haven* is to help others shine in their gifts and talents while teaching them to carry the torch ahead to the next generation so we don't lose the beauty of creation and its gift of life. As custodians of the earth, we are called to pass down all that we have been gifted with and we are also called to shine the light deep into the gully and guide others along the mystery of life.

Our assignments are small tasks that lead us to the ultimate goal in life that gives purpose, hope, vision, and strength in life, shining the light on the next generation to the wide open spaces of creativity by helping them to see their dreams being birthed and coming true, by not waiting till they get to heaven to enjoy this; but creating heaven on earth for all to come and drink this beauty and grace at the river called life.

When I chose to spend my hard-earned income on myself and follow the dreams in my heart, I started to discover a place of freedom and peace. For so much of my life, I was allowing negative thoughts and actions to stop me from living out of my heart's desires.

The Dark Room
Strategies that can help your dreams come alive and develop.

I am excited that my dreams are real. Even though some are only in the development stage, they are ready to go through the wet ink in the darkroom to be developed. They are coming to life one frame at a time.

As I take the time to write and create and develop the dreams in my heart of seeing others develop into their true nature and identify their creativity and see them come alive.

I am blessed to be a visionary who sees the images of life come together and settle into a beautiful pattern before my eyes, as each soul takes one step in front of the other allowing the negative images in their minds to be developed into beauty shining out of them for all to see.

Creating beautiful flowers in the garden of life!

My dreams springboard into reality as a speaker and influencer with my TV and podcast show and as a wholeness writing coach.

What are your dreams?

We all have dreams and creativity with a story to share, don't allow someone else to write it for you. Ask yourself what creative space are you going to develop where your needs are expressed and you shine and grow into your identity!

When you permit yourself to share your story, it brings healing and excitement to other people who need to hear it. My dad often said time stands still for nobody. God rest his soul. He is now at peace with family in heaven living his new life in Eternity.

I invite you to connect with me to see your life develop as we share **our stories** and help others heal along the journey.

4 Keys to help you live out the life of your dreams!

1.   You must focus on your goal and be single-minded with your choices and time.
2.   Take your dreams off the shelf and develop them and allow passion to be ignited in your life.
3.   Take the steps of faith and believe in yourself and write your story with grace and confidence.

4.   Don't ignore your heart's cries. Allow your dreams to thrive in your season with passion and purpose.

How Creative Writing Heals

Writing can be a massive healing for you and your reader. Becoming a published author brought me so much freedom in my heart and life. When I permitted myself to move into my creative writing it brought so much healing into my life on many levels.

Drafting my story has brought healing to the wounds of the past. It has given me a greater understanding of myself and allowed me to blossom.

As you permit yourself to share your story by expressing your dreams, this can bring healing to you and your readers on many levels.

Writing can help you cast down negative voices that want to rise in your head, from the hacklers and lies of the past to the fears of what the future may hold. Instead, focus on developing the gifts that make your heart sing.

Creative writing can bring a new level of freedom and joy. Allow yourself to express your God-given talents without boundaries and limits, free from the world and your mind. We all walk through dark seasons in life; it's how we travel through them that brings healing and freedom to us. I invite you to take the time to express your dreams and thoughts on paper. Doing this can open doors of healing and freedom to a wounded soul and an aching heart.

I have put aside years of pain and made my dreams of being a creative writer a reality. So now, I am achieving my heart cries that were buried for decades by sharing my voice on multiple platforms to help inspire others to create and see their lives transformed.

Becoming a published author has catapulted me into my dream goal of an #1 international bestselling author, speaker, TV and podcast host. I've allowed creativity to bring healing and freshness to my world by taking time to express my authentic self.

My Journey into Healing

My story focuses on moving into healing and how creative writing has brought joy and adventure to my life. Over the years, I have walked through many dark roads and valleys where I experienced deep grief and loss as my dreams to be a mother and carry my babies here on this earth never came to pass for me.

When I take the time to journal my thoughts and express myself with writing, this is an avenue that I use to help bring healing and hope to my world. For example, my book "Just Say

No" is a collection of inspirational stories from women about awakening your authentic self and highlights the magnitude of owning your power and living in abundance.

"Just Say No" is your guide to breaking free from negative mindsets, healing from past wounds, unlocking your potential, and creating the greatest impact in the lives of those with whom you connect.

I was challenged by God to share my own personal journey with the world. When I said yes to my dreams of becoming a published author and scripted my story sharing it with my friends and peers this brought another degree of healing and freedom to my heart and soul. As I started to unlock my grief and pain it morphed and transformed into a beautiful butterfly that gave me wings ready to take on a new expression in my world. Instead of feeling stuck and wrapped in a cocoon of grief my true identity now shines where I have more joy expressing my creativity with passion and gusto.

5 Healthy Keys to help you explore your creativity in a safe environment.

Creative lesson 1: Identity
Don't allow the negative voices of the past to dictate your future.

Keep in your own lane and don't allow the voices of the past to derail your dreams of achieving your creative goals.

Don't allow the demons of the past to stop you from achieving all your God-given dreams and talents. Don't hide your talent under a bushel by allowing fear to rule your future. This is not helpful. Shake it off and form healthy boundaries that allow you to follow your dreams and desires.

Creative lesson 2: Be Authentic
Feed your childlike spirit.

Dream big and bring to life your creative flow. Don't allow the cares of the world to crush your creativity. Be free to play like a child and allow the power of your mind to produce your visions.

Uproot the false narrative that may be hindering your growth to succeed and silence the voices in your head that stop you from achieving. Say YES to forming healthy habits that will allow you to achieve your creative flow.

Creative lesson 3: Mindset Matters
Self-care is an important part of the Journey.

Whether it is playing an instrument or taking a walk in the bush, allow your creative vibe to be birthed and flow. Or take a long hot bath to rest your weary bones with your favorite essential oils in bath salts. Taking the time to rest and breathe is a great way to set yourself up for healthy, creative juices to flow.

Creative lesson 4: Fall in love with You!
Silence the Voices of the Critics.

So many times, we allow the negative voices of the past to play like a broken record in our minds. We allow them to get stuck on repeat until it becomes etched in our subconscious and overrides the beauty and power of our Creator and the fabulous mind we are born with.

Give yourself permission to shine and create. Pick up a paintbrush and start creating. Reproduce that happy place where you are free to play and form shapes and designs. Allow that song that has been floating around in your head to be written down and become beautiful notes for all to hear and share.

Creative lesson 5: Be Courageous
Drink from the Cup of Courage.

Always allow yourself to refill your cup. Don't go around serving other people's dreams and visions if you find that this is crushing your authentic process. Learn to live in the moment and develop your creative lifestyle.

Spend time feeding your spirit of creativity so you have reserves to give to others by blocking out the voices in your head that are stopping you from achieving your goals.

Nurture your body with healthy food, rest, and learn how to ignore the cries of the world that have been driving you to distraction and just be.

The Reward

As a wholeness coach, speaker, publisher, bestselling author, and artisan, my journey of transformation has allowed me to come into my destiny. As a leader in helping women thrive not just survive, I have created a powerful platform with my TV and podcast show *The Thriving Woman*. I am building a successful business serving my clients with integrity and honesty helping them thrive in their seasons and drawing out their authentic creative selves.

I am taking daily steps to keep my health a priority. When I do this my self-esteem is balanced, and I draw others to myself and lead with grace and strength. I am grateful for the opportunity to live out my dreams with a creative supportive husband who stands at my side cheering me on in my adventures and artistic expression.

Life is a journey... Just like the waves of the ocean, it has its ups and downs. But as it says in Proverbs 3:5-6, NKJ "Trust in the Lord with all your heart and lean not on your own understanding; in all your ways submit to him, and he will make your paths straight." Keep believing in your dreams and trust that God has a plan for your life.

Fill in the blank.
I am created for _____ to _____ and _____.

Life is meant to be lived with creativity, enthusiasm, and spunk.
Always giving yourself time to explore your true identity.
~ Carmel Austin

Carmel Austin

Songs that inspired me to be courageous!
"Thrive" – Casting Crowns
"You Say" - Lauren Daigle
"April Sun in Cuba" – Dragon (first released in 1977).

Beach Life Dalmeny,
New South Wales

Balloon Fest 2023.
Canowindra New South Wales

Scenic Expression
The Three Sisters Blue Mountains
New South Wales, Australia

About the Author

Carmel Austin is an #1 International best-selling author, speaker, wholeness life coach, mentor, artisan, designer, and publisher. As the founder of Carmel's Garden, her coaching ministry that empowers women and families to transform their creative lives by connecting creativity and spiritual growth, she helps her clients gain the clarity, consistency, and confidence they need to share their God-given message with the world. As a certified wholeness writing coach, Carmel's passion is helping women and families grow in their creativity while growing spiritually.

Through her writing and coaching, Carmel shares her personal story of creativity and as a Wholeness Life Coach while getting "real" about life as a writer, coach, creator, and business owner. Her previously published works include *Just Say No: Dear Superwoman*. These have been co-author books where she partnered with other creatives around the globe. Carmel has her own TV and Podcast show 'The Thriving Woman' where she enjoys interviewing creatives and like-minded coaches. Tune into Spotify and listen to or watch her show.

In addition to her written published work, Carmel is a sought-after speaker and coach, offering workshops, exclusive group coaching training, and mentoring one-on-one coaching focused on living transformed lives and writing transformed creatively. Her compassionate, supportive approach offers a unique perspective on keeping balanced with healthy boundaries in life and creativity living from your authentic self.

When she's not writing or coaching, Carmel enjoys spending time with her family, walking her dog at the beach, camping, sitting around a campfire, and spending time with her grandchildren. Carmel loves trying out different forms of art and creating heirloom quilts for her family. Her positive energy and unwavering commitment to her mission make her a true inspiration and pillar of support for creatives, writers, and creatives everywhere.

Carmel loves to connect with other creatives helping and teaching them to grow, she has a passion to see others thrive in their season of life.

FIND ME:
Website: Carmel's Garden https://www.carmelsgarden.com/
Facebook: https://www.facebook.com/carmelsgarden/
https://www.facebook.com/carmel.austin1
Instagram:
https://www.instagram.com/carmelsgardenwholenesscoach

Schedule a free 30-minute Mind Mapping call with me where I can help you plan your next steps to become a published author.
https://calendly.com/carmelsgarden385/30min

Email: carmelsgardenpublish@gmail.com

The Artist Haven

It is only after you turn the negative into a positive that you can see the world for what it truly has to offer. In the next chapter, Dorease, a fellow photographer, talks about how she views the world from the lens of beauty, awe, and wonder.

Dedication

*The wonder seeker's "good eye" passed down from my sweet and lovely **Momma. Doris E. Haltom** is my lifelong cheerleader. Her artistic and creative expression endures with interior design, decorating and landscaping. Thus, it'd be natural to dedicate my entire manuscript to this artsy "creative" and gutsy 'Rodeo Queen' from yesteryear. Even so, I'm compelled to honor **"My Three Fathers,"** as well.*

*So, "hats off" to the blue-eyed blonde Horseman, Huntsman and Houndsman in Heaven ~ **Lawrence E. Berry** ~ a joyful braveheart who died as a young Father, and... to the loyal, diligent, gentle-spirited Horseman and Woodworking Craftsman ~ **Don C. Haltom** ~ who raised me well and loved me as his own. Finally, and most importantly, all glory goes to my **Heavenly Father** whose lavish love is from everlasting to everlasting. Each one of 'the fabulous four' influenced my faith journey on 'a road less traveled by.' Also, they each contributed significantly to my lifelong passion for horses, dogs and a 'grit and grace' lifestyle in the rural countryside.*

My wonder-graced heart will overflow with loving gratitude for 'the fabulous four', forevermore. ~Dorease

Art of a Wonder Seeker's Heart
A Photographer's Enduring Romance with Wonder

Dorease Rioux
The Victory for Purpose Coach

Woodland Park, Colorado, USA

"Gratitude is happiness doubled by wonder."
~ G.K. Chesterton [2]

The Day a Camera Saddled Up with a Wonder-Graced Heart

"One... two... three..."(CLICK)!

With my parents' forgotten old camera, I climbed up on the side of the horse trailer and pressed the shutter button. From this vantage point, I captured a moment in time as evening sunlight danced around in pool depths of warmest amber. The horse and I were connected soul to soul. His eye was an intuitive and knowing one that gazed back into mine.

A summer breeze stirred up dust with the wild and invigorating earthen smells of the National Rodeo. The fullness of spirited wonder swirled all around, just waiting for me to grab hold with gritty grace.

---

[2] Goodreads.com. (2023). Quotable Quotes. Retrieved from:
https://www.goodreads.com/quotes/386774-gratitude-is-happiness-doubled-by-wonder

At 8 years old, there was nothing about a horse that I didn't love... their herbal scent, the sighs and nickers they made and their soft, velvety muzzle that invited gentle touch. Sunset glistened from his coppery-red coat as he stood tethered beside the trailer. The weighty athlete almost thrummed with anticipation for his next go round in the big stadium arena that streamed with lights and riveting excitement. As a seasoned calf-roping horse, Buddy Joe Smith knew how to race against the clock and would deliver with his usual sureness.

The sorrel gelding had won my Daddy money, buckles and recognition over the years. Frequently, our family beamed with pride because Buddy Joe had gained the admiration of cowboys from around Texas and the South who wished the horse was theirs. Our own kind-natured horseman and his lead horse were a deeply bonded pair. They didn't care much about having names in lights but relished the adventures they shared together... with a well-worn saddle along for the ride.

My wonder-inspired photographic journey began with that single photo of a horse's gleaming eye. About 25 years later, I received a call one evening that Daddy had been out at the barn to do woodworking in his shop. With the pleasing scent of timber-dust drifting all around, he heard the usual hoof-knock on the back door and opened it so his faithful old friend could saunter up into the open space to enjoy the company of the master-woodworker as he created from old planks of oak and cedar.

The warm radiance of sunlit vespers wafted in through the barn window. Man and horse basked in the golden glow of camaraderie as familiar country-western ballads crooned from the shop-worn radio. You could almost see the musical notes-in-

serenade that floated gently away on sawdust... shimmering like woebegone-cowboys-in-miniature on their dream-like horses.

Later, Daddy went and fed Buddy Joe his evening grain. Afterwards, the rodeo cowboy lingered to watch his fine old horse mosey away to graze some more before darkness set in.

That was Buddy Joe Smith's last stand before he staggered, dropped and the glow of sunset faded from his warm-amber eyes caught on film so long ago by a wonder-graced little cowgirl.

An Americana Heritage Embossed with Gold

That simple childhood exploit became a springboard in my life. Passion would spur me on to make other photographs that would cause my heart to sing... snapshots that still take me inside soulful moments with a sense of golden wonder.

As an adult, I've loved and tended well to four horses of my own. Like I first did with Buddy Joe, they and their knowing eyes imprinted on my heart and, when the lighting was right, onto my camera roll too. I find beauty and wonder in the eyes of an equine because trust and friendship are spoken there.

Now, I close my eyes and warmly reminisce on my wholesome Americana roots... and how *God used the soul of a horse to ignite the artistic nature of a wee golden-haired lassie to capture wonder on film.* That was the day I became a dyed-in-the-wool shutterbug. Years later, I still am.

Broken Crayons Still Colour

As I grew up, *I never un-learned the bliss of wonder nor the curiosity and amazement that it spurred.* I could've easily outgrown it, but *I held onto the sweet nostalgia of wonder because it was like honeybee gold for a sentimental soul.*

My wonder-seeking capacity, along with my passion for creatively expressing it on film, were too precious to leave behind. So, I continued to explore and stay mindful of engaging in wonder throughout the years ahead.

My heartwarming habit of capturing beauty on film became increasingly pronounced after I fell headlong into the depths of deception. During that lengthy season, I repeatedly found myself in the throes of soul pain as I made my way through a shadowy serpentine labyrinth.

To explain... As an overly trusting young woman with a sunny outlook, I was easy prey. Thus, I was charmed into a convincing covert's snare. Those years should've been my most prolific, but I largely wasted them as I barely withstood the daily muck and mire in the conniver's carefully concealed catacombs. With the exception of cherished relationships on the periphery, I was stuck in a dark abyss with a *Jekyll-and-Hyde* personage.

After being lured in, I suffered silently in that controlling, double-dealing, destructive relationship where I was skillfully manipulated and repeatedly blind-sided with various types of abuse, jealous eruptions of rage, serial betrayals, persuasive falsehoods and other deceptive schemes. Being *an ever-hopeful "Pollyanna" optimist*, I continued to fall for the smooth-talker's countless convincing falsehoods over those years.

Furthermore, my Kingdom assignments were derailed as every hard hit brought detours with isolated grief and numerous varied losses. With each traumatic event, I chose to cling to my relationship with Jesus. In the darkness of despair, He was my refuge of safety... a faithful, shining light. Also, I was immensely comforted as I feasted in God's Word. I experienced how *"The*

Lord is close to the brokenhearted and saves those who are crushed in spirit." (Psalm 34:18 NIV)

Looking back, I find it astounding that I held fast to my rose-blooming depths of wonder, gratitude and joy. They were deeply interwoven in my heart like radiant ribbons of gold, braided with an ancient red cord.

Later, I would learn that **the creation of art transfers from the right brain to the processing center for grief.**

If art plays a part in healing the heart, then, that would explain why my camera had stayed in one hand and a well-worn Bible in the other. I never stopped creating art during those years marked with so many soul-pain wounds. I've no doubt **broken crayons still colour.**

Eventually, I broke free and fled those wastelands-in-disguise. I obeyed God's Word... thus, I forgave, blessed, prayed for and graciously shook the dungeon debris from my feet as I left the crafty schemer *"...to their own devices."* (Proverbs 1:31 ESV)

Over the decades, I never disclosed the despicable and destructive things the grinning player did. I should've. They continued to be an unprincipled, 'woe-is-me', deceiving individual who never deserved my silence then or now.

Although I have no feelings nor respect for that darkly troubled soul, to this day, I still have no desire to expose them. I gave them over to the Lord long ago.

A Crown of Beauty for Ashes

Because the Lord sees His children brimming with dignity, worth and value, He sweetly gave me a *"crown of beauty for ashes."* (Isaiah 61: 3 NLT)

God specializes in the restoration of broken things. During my brave heart venture toward the Promised Land, the Holy Spirit tenderly sorted through the shattered damage of my soul and He restored my life from the beat-down, broken pieces. As with a **Kintsugi** pottery vase, the Master Artist endearingly fashioned me back together. He applied gleaming gold where gaping wounds had been.

To get to where I am today, I leaned into the Lord and did the work to heal from narcissistic abuse and betrayal traumas. Also, I reclaimed my identity and self-worth, along with my Kingdom purpose, gifts and calling. I chose to rescript my future with fresh vision and to joyously embrace a restored lifestyle of freedom.

Now, as *"The Victory for Purpose" Coach*, I continue to *"reap with songs of joy"* (Psalm 126: 5 AMP) as I help other Kingdom Believers get unstuck to cross over into the Promised Land too. It's heart-warming to walk alongside as they discover their grace gifts, callings and purpose.

A Tapestry of Grace Gifts

A grace gift can be something as simple as holding a fluffy one-day-old Easter Egger chick named "Dolly Parton"... or as simple as your favorite song that plays on the radio three times in a day... or when a resplendently adorned dragonfly lights onto your hand. It's when you respond with gratitude that it becomes a gift.

The grace gifts I most want to address are inherent, God-given ones. I was born as a **visionary leader** and **encourager** with **a Shepherd's heart.** Also, I'm a **'creative'** and carry innate talents for various **'art'** forms.

I was born with these gifts to inspire and empower others so I would fulfill my Kingdom purpose, for His glory. So, my various grace gifts aren't really about me, but they're to help others and bring glory to God. (I Peter 4:10)

I believe **every person is fashioned with a measure of creativity** because we're made in God's image (spirit, soul and body). He is the Master Creator… and as followers of Christ, He lives in us by His Holy Spirit! Thus, **everyone has the capacity within themselves for some type of creative expression**. You simply have to step out in faith to try something that interests you and let your imagination soar. It's better to attempt something compelling than to not use your creativity at all.

So, what might it look like for you to embrace *creativity? Doodling perhaps… or decorating your parlor with finesse… or fashioning together a tastefully dazzling party outfit?* When you apply creativity, you share glimpses into who you are.

When your heart is engaged with the Father's heart, your gifts and creative expression take on greater shine because your perspective enlarges. He actually offers you the capacity to see as He sees. For me, it's wholesome goodness to marvel with gratitude over the novelty I see, then to press the shutter button with amazement. When you develop and use your God-given gifts, they become your gift back to Him.

God wants you to use your grace gifts to bless others and bring Him glory. Your gifts will make room for you. Even so, it's not really about you, but about walking in your unique God-given purpose with pure motives and intentions that please Him.

Art of a Wonder Seeker's Heart

One of the ways I help others is through *creative writing.* Penning inspirational messages is a glorious, creative preoccupation and an art form that consumes me with a deep sense of fulfillment.

Furthermore, I'm told I was *"born with 'a good eye' for the 'visual' arts."* Some of my *'visual'* artistic gifts have included... *amateur photography, interior decorating, scenic set design, and, more recently, where I place paint with the arrangement of elements onto a painter's canvas.*

I've found if you're inherently gifted with "a good eye" in one of the *'visual'* grace gifts, then all four and more should overlap to come naturally for you because having *"an innate good eye"* plays a vital role in all *'visual'* art forms.

Co-create with God

Let us zoom in on **"photography"** which, for some, has the potential to be a creative *'visual'* art form that's more than just an impassioned interest or pleasurable hobby.

Similar to other creative 'visual' pursuits, **photography has two distinct sides**. First, there's the intuitive *"inherent good eye"* side with high creative 'visual' artistic ability. These photographers are naturally *"picture smart."* They were born that way. Allegedly, it's published in the literature that roughly 5-10% are **born with 'an innate good eye.'**

Then, there's the other side of photography. It involves **the technical, mechanized elements** which can be "**learned**" by just about anyone.

An art mentor clarified that *you can be 'Creative' to some degree without being 'Artistic'; however,* **a true 'Artist' who, also, carries a high degree of 'Creativity,' makes for a significantly gifted Artist.**

At a tender young age, artistic pursuits and creative expression came naturally for me. I've been told by a few credible experts that I was **born with "a good eye"** for the *'visual'* arts. I intuitively seem to understand detail, lighting, composition, spatial relations, background dynamics and how to quickly frame a photo.

Over a four-day women's retreat a longtime Professor of Art & Design, from a major State University in America's Heartland, sat beside me. As this academic art expert looked through my informal, raw, un-edited snapshots, she told me I had been *"born with a good eye."* It confirmed many things. I wept in amazement as *a lot was brought to the light* over our days together.

It might've only been an astounding coincidence, but I believe it was divinely orchestrated. The Lord wants to impart truth to His beloved whether it's honest feedback we desire to hear or not. Either way, **"truth" shines light onto blind spots and brings reality to center-stage.** My learnings over those days, at the art professor's side, proved to be another landmark event in my life.

Sometimes when I look back at the few photos taken on any given day, I often see **divinely inspired works of art** as an outflow of communion with the Lord. In my opinion, my photos probably wouldn't stand out on a search-engine site unless they were color-saturated and post-processed with other heavy-handed touch-ups to garner notice.

Regardless, *it becomes creative worship* when I tune in... spirit-to-Spirit... with a heart of worship. That's when I become inspired to create art with divine imagination through my soul, hands and camera lens. For me, it's *fresh and living art that nourishes my spirit... it reflects my soul, somewhat like a mirror for anyone else who might truly "see."*

Even so, I confess I've never enjoyed **the mechanized, technical aspects of "***learning***" the equipment, post-processing and other practical, methodical skills that can be acquired.** *For a dominantly-right-brained personality who's adventurous, optimistic and expressive... "the techy side" of photography is restrictive and draining. If making instinctively perceptive photos is like honey for my soul, the mechanized side of photography is like sipping on red-wine vinegar.*

Most artists will concur that having *'an innate good eye' for intuitive photographic composition, etc, trumps all the bells-and-whistles of camera gear and "learning" the techy, mechanical side of* photography.

The masterful photographers are those who are golden with both the innate "good eye" and the "learned" side. Whether or not we are one of those golden photographers, it's okay. We're still ***invited into God's unfolding story of wonder.*** Let us respond, relish and enjoy the pilgrimage of co-creation.

Become as a Little Child

In late summer of 1999, my then-good-friend and I went on dozens of hikes together throughout Arizona. On our first adventure, Tim was curiously affected by my evident childlike wonder and gratitude. It was *"my normal,"* but to him it was new. He was captivated to watch me explore nature with my camera.

As was the norm, I repeatedly stopped during our hike to exclaim with amazement and to take single-shot photos of whatever caught my eye and brought me pleasure.

With admiration, Tim conveyed that he had *never known anyone to notice and inspect details that seemed commonplace.* He appreciated how I *enjoy subtleties that most people consider ordinary or uninteresting.* Tim brought to light that I *look for and discover beauty in things that most people overlook and walk past.*

There would be countless more nature hikes shared with Tim during our friendship and, later, during *our wonder-filled courtship.* He would continue to acknowledge ***my heart on display as a wonder-seeking shutterbug with God's praises on my lips.***

On Resurrection Sunday in 2001, I married my good man in a late-1880's-style church in Arizona. He still waits for me when I stop to immerse myself in fresh amazement on our *'wonder-walk-abouts.'* Tim knows I don't want to miss out on anything the Lord wants to reveal; thus, *I'll never be one to wander past the wonders.*

Beauty. Awe. Wonder.

Most people marvel in **awe** as they behold moonlit mountainscapes blanketed in snow... a lush, scenic valley as viewed from a cliff... or a tumbling waterfall that cascades down a mountainside through a forest adorned in dappled sunlight... yet, they don't **become wonder-struck by the beauty** of the less-obvious, more-diminutive ecosystems that teem with life on the floor of a forest, for example.

I safe-guarded my **wonder-tinted lenses** as I grew up. So, I still like to lean in to **see the potential for the extraordinary in the ordinary**... and to notice novelty and beauty as I meander. Whether my inspiration is one of awe, wonder or both... for me, it's not as much about what I see through the camera viewfinder, but the way I see it and how I feel about the encounter in my heart. As Henry David Thoreau said... it's not what you look at that matters... it's what you **see**.

Awe comes easy for almost everyone, but you cannot pretend a sense of **wonder** for very long. It's something authentic which springs up from within your soul. It's *'a road less traveled by.'*

Thieves of Wonder

In Tim's case and in that of many others, maybe the art of wonder was lost over time because it was perceived as 'childish' instead of *'childlike.'* Perhaps many assume they should grow out of 'childlike' fascination and become 'adultish.'

Secondly, living in **the daily grind** with a mundane routine or working a **high-pressure** job can gradually beat one down into an outlook that's lack-lustre.

Thirdly, lingering **hurts and hard feelings** like resentment, unforgiveness and bitterness weave together a dim-and-darkened soul which blocks sunlit wonder.

Finally, another reason for not living with the art of a wonder-graced heart is **'boredom'**... **being 'bored'** or **'boring.'** I've heard it said that *"only boring people get bored."* No doubt, we tend to **see** things as **we** are; however, I'm convinced anyone can choose to shift their perspective to see things in a fresh light. Thus, I believe there's no room for boredom when a person is authentically engaged with wonder, gratitude and creative expression.

What a wonderful world

The Creator of the Universe is not a commonplace artist. His creative expression abundantly endures and enriches. Based on our response, He actually grants His beloved latitude to see as He sees. Perspectives will transform during heart-to-heart engagement with the Lord... like a butterfly emerging from a cocoon.

Childlike wonder... and a grateful heart that wells up in worship... have given me ongoing access to dimensions of God that are fresh and vivid.

Additionally, my hobby photography is a reflection of the creative art that springs up from my worshipful, wonder-graced heart.

As both *a wonder seeker* and a *photographer who engages with creative expression*, it's a habit to capture my delight on camera. When I freeze frame that single-grace moment, it reveals how I see the world around me. *However, it's immeasurably more wondrous when I'm mindfully aware of His presence too.*

My lifelong romance with wonder is wholesome and good, but how much more must it please the Lord when I rejoice in Him and delight in His creation? It's something special that Elohim and I share together.

I want you to experience that too. So does the Creator of Heaven and earth!

"The entire universe stands on tiptoe, yearning to see the unveiling of God's glorious sons and daughters!" (Romans 8:19 TPT)

A Shutterbug's Enduring Romance with Wonder

As I reminisce, I consider how I've lived my life with a sensitivity for sensory experiences and heart-full impressions as I've sought to stay aware of the refreshing beauty of nature and God's creative wonders all around. However, I realize that living with a deep sense of wonder is not a foundational, essential truth for a Christian's life. Likewise, creative pursuits aren't either.

Even so, they can become resurrectional facets in our lives. I've known, firsthand, that creative expression plays a part in healing our wounded hearts.

My enduring romance with wonder is because the Lord knows my heart's desires and His faithfulness is everlasting. Thus, as His beloved daughter who notices and responds with gratitude, I keep wonder stirred up in my heart. Those golden embers are always aglow, but it's *my choice* to fan them often and offer up worship, like fragrant incense, before the Lord.

After all these years, it's still *a deep-rooted response to the hum of life* for me to pause, photograph and partake in the details… to touch… smell… listen… marvel… imagine… and offer up thanksgiving to Elohim… the giver of wonder to all who choose to "see" and respond with thankfulness. I wish this for you, as well.

I hope this illuminating and whimsical share from my wonder-graced heart has inspired **you** to awaken a sense of childlike wonder, too, along with artistic and creative expression in your own journey. If so, will you find me online, share your story and let me cheer you along on *"a road less traveled by?"*
With Wonder, Gratitude and Joy… Dorease Rioux

 *Dorease Rioux*

"To create with the Holy Spirit is more about the process than the product… more about the intention than the outcome. It's about cultivating ears to hear, eyes to see, and senses to feel what God is saying and doing within your world. Then, to respond through your chosen creative process."
~ Matt Tommey[3]

---

[3] Tommey, M. (2021). Prophetic Art: A Practical Guide for Creating with the Holy Spirit. Independently published.

*"The Band of Brothers"... **Caperten, Shiloh and Sully**... graze together in an alpine mountain meadow of wildflowers at "Grit and Grace Ranch of the Highlands"* ~ The Colorado Rockies, USA.

It's a precious gift to gaze into a horse's eye... to connect soul-to-soul.
This is Shiloh blanketed in Autumn sun glow.
He's a stunning and regal Tennessee Walker ~ "movie star" material!
Grit and Grace Ranch of the Highlands ~ The Colorado Rockies, USA

Stir up your childlike sense of wonder and delight in God's beauty all around. Pause and see the movement of sun-washed bark contrasted with vibrant colors and velvety textures that blanket an alpine forest floor in the high country of the Rocky Mountains. ~ Grit and Grace Ranch of the Highlands
~ The Colorado Rockies, USA

About the Author

Over several decades, **Dorease Rioux** has been a plane-hopping, award-winning businesswoman in Corporate America, a Registered Nurse in Critical Care before that and a Ministry Leader throughout most of her adult life. Dorease is also a singing shutterbug with a *innate good eye* for photography.

She carries a perceiving awareness for creative expression as an amateur artist in several fields. Additionally, Dorease is a Kingdom-minded empowerment coach, soon-to-be-4-times-published author, media guest and inspirational speaker with a compassionate heart and passionate style. Dorease speaks on topics like the power of forgiveness, narcissistic abuse, betrayal trauma, healthy boundaries, how to fulfill your Kingdom destiny with purpose and with *eternal rewards* in mind. She also teaches others how to prepare now for *'grid down'*.

Dorease was born as an inspirational leader and an encourager with a Shepherd's heart. As **The Victory for Purpose Coach,** she helps others get unstuck so they can move forward to reclaim their purpose with fresh vision and fulfill their Kingdom destiny. Dorease and Tim enjoy their *"Grit and Grace Homestead in the Land of Goshen."* They live near her beloved parents, have 7 delightsome dogs and, as you might imagine, Dorease keeps her trusty Fuji-Film camera and Bible within easy reach.

FIND ME:
Dorease invites you to learn more about her ***"Crowned for Purpose"*** Coaching Program. **To schedule a free 30-minute *"Victory For Purpose"* call,** you can send a Direct Message via Facebook **Messenger.**
Facebook:
https://www.facebook.com/dorease.rioux
Private Facebook Group:
"Wear the CROWN. Fulfill the CALL."
https://www.facebook.com/groups/529654824795621/?ref=share_group_link&exp=9594
Email: Dorease.Empowers@gmail.com

The Artist Haven

When you feel broken inside, you can still pull a crayon from your pocket to colour the world. With that broken blue or pink crayon in your hand, I hope you'll turn to and trust the Lord with your pocket of hurts. I know firsthand that He wants to heal your brokenness, give your life back to you and restore your God-ordained destiny. Stephanie understands this as well. In the next chapter, "The Black Crayon," Stephanie shows us what expressing her emotions through her art looked like.

Dedication

To my three children, Abigail, Nathaniel and Tabitha. I pray you always are free to express yourself creatively. I pray you always are brave enough to color outside the lines and not keep your creative gifts tucked away in the box.

Always remember that you are fearfully and wonderfully made to do great things! May you always reach for the stars and be confident to pursue your creative dreams! I pray that each of you stays curious and adventurous and that you never use sight of your "child-like wonder!"

And to those of us with creative influence over the future generation- May we always seek to create an environment for our children to flourish as God created them to be! ~ Stephanie

Your children are not a masterpiece that you create.
They are their own masterpieces creating themselves,
And you have been given the privilege of watching them be the artist. ~J. Warren Welch[4]

---

[4] Welch, J. W. (2021). Facebook post. Retrieved from:
https://www.facebook.com/j.warren.welch/posts/373005057514810/

The Black Crayon

Stephanie Miller
Writing & Spiritual Growth Coach

Atlanta, Georgia, USA

"Creativity takes courage."
~ Henri Matisse[5]

"Is that how you really feel?" the group facilitator asked me while handing me a black crayon. I had drawn a lovely picture of a house sitting on green grass and a sun with a smiley face. Grabbing the crayon from her hand, I immediately started scribbling violently with it over the picture I had just made.

Pressing down so hard with that black crayon that my hand hurt, I could see the shine start to appear over the paper as the black started to hide the colourful picture. I couldn't stop at just one or two black scribbles; once she handed me the black crayon, it was as if something was unleashed inside me. Once she handed me that black crayon, all bets were off; it was like the floodgates had been opened, and she granted me the permission I never knew I needed. The permission to stop pretending and stop trying to please everyone else. Permission to stop trying to hide behind colourful pictures of houses and smiley face suns. Permission rooted in the acceptance of who I

---

[5] Matisse, H. (n.d.). Retrieved from: https://www.henrimatisse.org/henri-matisse-quotes.jsp

was and, more importantly, the acknowledgment of my emotions.

I'm not sure the girl facilitating that program really understood the impact it had on me. She gave me permission to express my truest self in colour form. She gave me permission to feel how I felt. Black isn't necessarily a go-to colour when you're trying to draw a pretty picture, but it is a go-to colour when you are capturing the complexity of your feelings. The colour black results from the absence or the complete absorption of visible light. In other words, black can represent a void, or it can represent the full spectrum of colour. Looking back, I think colouring with black helped me to express the void I felt, but it also summed up the complexity of my feelings and the misunderstanding I experienced.

This was quite the breakthrough for a 6-year-old girl who had been struggling to handle her emotions in the dysfunctional household that was her reality. While it may not seem like a big deal to others, the invitation to stop hiding my emotions and instead express them through creative means has been vital to me as a writer and creative. The permission she granted me by offering the black crayon started a chain of events in my life that I carry with me still today.

I started going to this program aptly titled "Colour your feelings" once a week because my mum would go to Al-Anon, where my brother and I would go to "color our feelings." I don't have a vivid memory of this experience in terms of where we went, how long we went for, or even the facilitator of the group. But I do remember the freedom I suddenly felt once I started colouring with the black crayon.

Around the time I started attending those meetings, my parents had recently separated. I struggled to understand what was going on and had a hard time processing their separation. In my happy picture, I was drawing what I wished was true. I desired to have a happy, loving, warm household with a united family, but my reality was far from picture-perfect.

The "happy picture" was the first step I made to colour my feelings. It was not until the third session that I drew that picture or even picked up a crayon. The other times I just sat there. Was it defiance? Maybe. Was it some form of resistance? Definitely. I've always been the girl who, once the tears come, it's hard to get them to stop. The girl who, once I've allowed myself to feel, feel deeply and express those thoughts and feelings in a variety of ways.

This experience was the first time I was exposed to the fact that pain can be beauty, something I have carried with me ever since that moment. The black crayon opened the door to allow me to process my emotions that day and paved the way for me to continue to use creative outlets to process my strong feelings as a child, then as a teenager, and now as an adult.

As a teenager, I traded those crayons for a pen and a journal. It was during the times when my parents were yelling at each other, or my house felt so unstable that I retreated to my room and curled up with my journal and pen. I turned to poetry to help me process the wave of emotions I was experiencing.

I wrote several poems as a teenage girl. Poems about feeling misunderstood, poems about desiring love and attention and affection from my father, poems about breakups with boys (that were the end of the world at the time but now seem trivial in hindsight). Whatever I was feeling and whatever depth of emotion I was experiencing, I turned into words on paper. These words mattered greatly to me because they captured my heart. I had no poetic conventions to follow; I just followed my feelings and what I needed to express in that moment.

Ernest Hemingway said, "There is nothing to writing. All you do is sit down at a typewriter and bleed."[6] And that's exactly what I did. When I wanted to feel particularly expressive, I turned to music to keep me focused on my emotions and the experience.

The same song played on repeat over and over and again. As I held onto each word, it fueled my writing. Each lyric so poignantly connected my thoughts with the words I was trying to express. My writing was always premeditated by an emotional event that happened to me.

I tried to capture my emotions and express them on paper. I also sought to discover myself through writing. Who was I? I hoped that my writing would show me who I really was, just like the picture I marked with the black crayon showed me how I was really feeling.

If I'm being honest, a part of me thinks that writing is the safest form of creativity and expression. As we place words on the page, there is flexibility to make corrections and adjustments (and a million revisions) until you get it right. I'm less critical of my writing because a word can be erased and deleted without a trace. But in painting, it's not so easy to undo an over-zealous paint brush stroke that changes the entire landscape of your picture. Those mistakes, or "happy little accidents," as the late

---

[6] Brainy Quote. (2023). Ernest Hemingway Quotes. Retrieved from: https://www.brainyquote.com/quotes/ernest_hemingway_384744

artist Bob Ross called them, connect our creative awareness to our creative experience.

Creative awareness comes from giving ourselves permission to create. This first starts with the understanding that creativity matters because it isn't just something we do but rather who we are. We are more than just individuals that sometimes like to dabble in art; creativity is part of our identity. We have been created to create because God, our creator Himself, made us in His image. So, God created mankind in his own image, in the image of God he created them; male and female he created them. (Genesis 1:27 NIV)

And He didn't just create us, He created ALL things, and everything He created was good. God saw all that he had made, and it was very good. And there was evening, and there was morning—the sixth day. (Genesis 1:31 NIV)

If we have been created to create good things, why do so many of us decide instead to stuff our creative desires in a box and only take them out when we think we've earned the right to do so?

If this creativity is tied so closely to who we are and who we have been created to be, then what causes us to lose sight of that part of ourselves?

For me, it was the pressure and expectation I placed on myself that was also encouraged by others close to me. Slowly, I stopped painting, drawing, and colouring as a little girl because it never resulted in the love and praise that I was so thirsty for. I wanted so desperately to be seen and acknowledged that I tried to mold my love of writing into more acceptable forms. My writing changed from poetry and short stories to essays and academic papers. I conformed to what others wanted, but I lost myself in the process.

While I always have had an affinity for writing, there is something undeniably satisfying about picking up a crayon and putting it to paper. Feeling the paintbrush between your fingers as you stroke the canvas, as, before you know it, an array of colour appears. I would not say that I'm "good" at painting, but I've learned to stop trying to be.

My friend, the goal of painting, writing, drawing, sculpting, sewing, and any other artistic activity you can think of is not to produce a polished result; it's to surrender to the creative process. In our surrender to the creative process, instead of our obsession with the outcome, we find peace. When we create from the place of peace, there is freedom. Our souls are at rest pursuing our craft instead of at war over the perfect words to use to describe a scene or the right way to paint a flower.

To really get to the place of freedom while creating, we need to get back to seeing our art as a form of emotional expression. If you think about it, we don't pursue creativity; rather, creativity pursues us. Operating in our truest creative potential, we are not concerned about where we are going but focused on the journey. We are in tune with who we are and what we are feeling in that moment.

During the times I coloured my feelings, I was connecting to how I was feeling in that moment.

During the times I wrote my poetry, I was connecting to how I was feeling in that moment.

During the times I journal and blog, I am connecting with how I am feeling in that moment.

I may not like it; I may not understand it, but I acknowledge it.

It is when we don't allow ourselves to acknowledge where we are and how we are feeling that these things fester and can cause problems like anxiety, depression, and even addiction. It's when we place pressure and expectations on ourselves, our creativity, and our art that we can begin to lose sight of whom we were originally created to be.

We were not created to devalue ourselves, wish we were somebody different, or wish we could do something different. We were created to be our authentic selves and create from that place of awareness and acceptance.

Each of our creative journeys is vastly different. This is on purpose. The Bible says we were fearfully and wonderfully made; this means that we are each unique, and the way we operate in our God-given creative potential looks different for all of us.

I'm not going to lie; coming to terms with this new understanding of myself caused quite a stir of identity within me. I started to question if this is who I've always been or if it was whom I was becoming. As I wrestled with this ongoing thought, suddenly, clarity came to mind.

I think the answer lies in my "black crayon" encounter:

When I picked up that black crayon and started colouring that paper, I didn't have the final result in mind. I had my immediate emotional release in mind. I had the process and experience in mind instead of the outcome. In that moment, I was free to be who I was and feel what I felt, even as a little girl. In that moment, even as I fervently scribbled, I embodied my truest creative self.

As a thirty-something adult now with three children of my own, I make emotional expression and creative freedom a regular practice in my house. I encourage my children to use colours that express how they feel, show them pictures of faces that illustrate different emotions, and give them crayons and markers, colouring books, and blank pieces of paper to use.

They create. They show up to the blank page, not worried about what the final drawing or colouring will look like. I'm teaching them to be ok with colouring outside the lines or choosing unconventional colours to represent the characters or objects in their colouring books. I'm teaching them that conformity has no place in creativity.

All the while reminding myself of the same. Creativity is our expression of self in the moment. In the simplest form, creativity is who we are, not what we do.

And if that means one of my children wants to use only the black crayon one day, you better believe that I'll be the one to hand it to them. Then it will be my turn to ask them, "Is that how you really feel?"

Reflection:

I encourage you to think back on your creative journey. Can you identify your own "black crayon" moment? Recall the moments that you experienced creative awareness and creative identity. Or, if you haven't yet, I encourage you to write out all the reasons (obstacles) that are stopping you from stepping into your God-given creativity.

From your list of identified obstacles, ask God in prayer to remove those blocks that are hindering your creative potential. Then release it over to God and pick up a paint brush, crayon, marker, pen and paper, clay, (really anything you can get your hands on) and create. Don't think about it, just do it!

Need more help dealing with your nasty inner critic? Check out my free guide below that is proven to help you stop the cycle of "stinkin' thinking"' so you can move forward in your creative journey!

Praying for you and cheering you on!

Stephanie

The Ultimate Muse

Sometimes the muse just won't appear
The words won't flow, the page is bare,
And though you try to Imaginate,
Try as you might, you remain stuck, unable to create.

You sit and stare, and ponder deep
And hope that inspiration soon will leap,
But as the minutes tick on by,
Your hopes for creative flow are starting to die.

Doubt begins to creep in,
The fear that you've lost your creative kin,
And you're a washed-up "has-been,"
Afraid you'll never find your spark again.

The weight of this discouragement
Leaves you feeling so forlorn,
And you wonder if it's worth the time,
Perhaps it's better to stop trying to be artistically reborn.

But deep down in your heart you know,
That art and words will always flow,
Though it seems elusive now,
The muse will come back, somehow.

You know how, you really do,

You remind yourself who you are in Christ,
How valuable you are to Him,
And the unique creative purpose He has for you.

So you take a deep breath, say a prayer, clear your mind,
And let yourself become unconfined.
Soon enough, the words will come
And your creative desires will be realigned.

You are not being buried under the weight of creative
discouragement,
Rather you are being planted.
May we never take this feeling,
Which is necessary for our creative growth, for granted.

So let us create, let us grow.
God will guide our steps,
And lead us on our creative path,
For this I know.

So we let go, and we release.
We remind ourselves His timing is perfect.
We trust God to work in us and through us,
To create His masterpiece.

About the Author

Stephanie Miller is a Christian best-selling author, speaker, and writing and spiritual growth coach. As the founder of Butterfly Beginnings, a coaching ministry that empowers women to transform their creative lives by connecting creativity and spiritual growth, she helps her clients gain the clarity, consistency, and confidence they need to share their God-given message with the world. As a certified spiritual growth coach and writing coach, Stephanie has a passion for helping women of faith grow in their creativity while growing spiritually.

Through her writing, Stephanie shares her personal story of creative and spiritual growth while getting "real" about the messiness of motherhood as a writer and business owner. Her previously published works include *The Butterfly Blueprint: How to Renew Your Mind and Grow Your Faith*. She also has been a co-author of several other books, including "I Am Enough in Christ" devotional and workbook, "Where Grace Found Me: Real Life Stories of Women of Faith", and "I Quit: Stories and Strategies to Help You Let Go of What No Longer Serves You."

In addition to her written published work, Stephanie is a sought-after speaker and coach, offering workshops and one-on-one coaching focused on living transformed (spiritual growth) and writing transformed (creative growth). Her compassionate, supportive approach offers a unique perspective on spiritual growth and creativity.

When she's not writing or coaching, Stephanie enjoys spending time with her family, working out, and trying out different forms of art. Her positive energy and unwavering commitment to her mission make her a true inspiration and pillar of support for Christian writers and creatives everywhere.

FIND ME:
Website: www.butterfly-beginnings.com
Facebook: www.facebook.com/stephaniemillercoach
Instagram: www.instagram.com/stephaniemillercoach
Email: stephanie@butterfly-beginnings.com
Schedule a Call: https://calendly.com/stephanie-miller-hw/20-minute-discovery-coaching-call
Free Gift for client: How to Use Faith-Based Frameworks to Make Real Writing Progress
 www.butterfly-beginnings.com/freebie

The Artist Haven

Working on leaving your creative mark on the world is also a passion of my fellow co-author, Sarah. Adjusting to her circumstances, she has been able to fuel her creative dreams. Her story is inspiring and encouraging and serves as a powerful reminder to "keep on keeping on" because a breakthrough in your creativity is often just a few steps away!

Dedication

To My Sweet Man, this is for you.

*Thank you for chipping away at my stony
hard exterior to find the beauty within,
transforming my idea of normal, and
walking with me daily as I learn what true freedom is.
~Sarah*

A Blank Page

Granny Mac
Strongly Justice Oriented,
Curious Explorer

West Otago, New Zealand

*"It is not the critic who counts... the credit belongs to the man who is actually **in the arena**, who spends himself in a worthy cause; who, at the best, knows, in the end, the triumph of high achievement, and who, at the worst, if he fails, at least he fails while daring greatly, so that his place shall never be with those cold and timid souls who knew neither victory nor defeat."*
~Theodore Roosevelt[7]
Speech at the Sorbonne, Paris, April 23, 1910

Have you ever noticed when you sit down with a fresh sheet of paper how hard it is to write something fabulous?

I was in the car talking with my Sweet Man when inspiration hit. We were talking about another project I have in hand at the moment and I was expressing my frustration with a Fresh Sheet of Paper and how that Blank Page seemed to be a

---

[7] The Theodore Roosevelt Center at Dickinson University. (n.d.) "The Man in the Arena." Address at the Sorbonne in Paris, France. "Citizenship in a Republic" at the Sorbonne in Paris. 23April1910. Retrieved from: https://www.theodorerooseveltcenter.org/Blog/Item/The%20Man%20in%20the%20Arena

"Wall of Awful," and therefore seemingly insurmountable when looked at as a whole.

With so many ideas struggling to get out, to be expressed, explored and expounded upon, finding one and sticking with it was more challenging than it seemed at first glance.

"It is not the critic who counts..."

A blank page has the power to intimidate in ways that trigger that sinking feeling you may have had at school where you were tasked with writing an essay, together with the ice-cold certainty that you couldn't write a thing - you didn't know where to start...

But what is the actual problem? Is it the fear of putting something down in writing that strangles our creativity or is it the fear of not getting "it" right? Perhaps it might be the fear of being judged on the results of the words sprawled across the page, spider-like, somewhat dyslexic and drowned in ink, but then again, this is the modern world and we tend to type more than write...

What if... what if we could approach the task with the image of a benevolent someone who is delighted to read whatever we write simply because we've been brave enough to put "pen to paper" and express ourselves in writing? What if that person being hungry for our words, is seen as encouraging rather than daunting? What if that person is longing for our perspective of a shared experience, so that theirs may be richer?

"... the credit belongs to the man who is actually
in the arena,"

What if instead of self-abasement we could be bold and brave with our thinking and dare to share those thoughts with someone who matters?

What if in expressing yourself via the written word, you set someone else free from thinking/feeling that they're all alone... that no one cares nor gives a damn? What if... what if by sharing the thoughts upon which you ruminate, you provide for someone else a more easily digested truth?

A Blank Page is an invitation to an as-yet unexplored arena whereby you are the trainer, your words are the horse, and someone else is the rider who brings home the Gold Medal.

Imagery is thick with potential, viscous as honey straight from the hive, full of healing, antibacterial effects and every bit as sticky sweet. The soporific result seems worth the effort of extricating it. Especially when it brings profound healing...

The words I write are no longer about me, it's you I see, and with this sudden transformation of perspective, I am no longer bound by my own inadequacy, rather I long to reach out, to tend your wounds instead of my own.

Together God and I are co-creating something rather wonderful actually. With the flavours of my life permeating each word presented with Michelin-like attention nuanced with experience, hemmed with prayer and stitched together with love to minister deeply to you...

This then is the effect of a once Blank Page now intimately acquainted with colour both oppositional in its composition and ministering in its application.

"... who spends himself in a worthy cause;"

God chose me for this task. He knows who He is looking for and He knows that there is something in me that will connect with you in the place you're at and give you what you're looking for. Perhaps it's hope that there is a way through, that it won't always be like this - there is (hope) and it won't be (always like this). Be brave and connect with those who can accompany you on your journey and together we'll make it to the other side of this season, wiser, older and probably with a few more grey hairs than we had before.

My dear friend Rose told me once that "It would be okay. I don't know what okay looks like, but it will be okay." I held onto that for a long time, believing in her wisdom, until I found my own. Now I have this to share from my hard-earned wisdom: "God knows the beginning from the end and He holds all the messy bits in the middle. It may have taken us by surprise, but He knows the way through."

What this means is that I can trust Him, or I could try it my own way: pig-headed, bullish, stubborn, ridden with pain, laced with agony and misunderstanding, tormented with fear... Or, I could boldly come alongside Him and say, "Can You please hold my hand through this?"

"... who, at the best, knows, in the end, the triumph of high achievement,"

Here's what I've learned. In spite of our technological and medical advances, there is nothing that can replace an amputation of the heart - which is what happens when we lock ourselves up with bitterness and anger - save for a loving Saviour who is intimately involved with us, at the level we allow Him to be; bringing His skin into the game of our life, who says, "I've got you."

When will you stop resisting Him?

I'm not!

Really? He wants you to have peace and instead, you keep yourself awake at night churning over and over the things that have been said and done in the PAST.

How's that working out for you?

Have you changed anything through your agonised ruminations?

Have you made yourself a better person?

Has all the criticism helped you figure out how to be a more excellent version of yourself?

But, if I let Him in, then none of my pain matters!

If you let Him in, then you'll find that your pain matters very much. He hurts every bit as much as you do about this situation. His heart, believe it or not, was the first to break when that thing happened, but He cannot and will not interfere with Free Will. Not even when someone imposes their Free Will on you because that is not who He is.

"... whose face is marred by dust and sweat and blood; "

God didn't take away Jesus' Free Will when He submitted Himself to the Cross. He willingly allowed Himself to be treated appallingly so that He could connect with the one who needed someone to understand what they've been through. He submitted to treasonous behaviour which ultimately signed His death warrant, He has suffered, cried, agonised and experienced things that we have endured so that you could look into His face and KNOW, that He knows, He gets it and He wants to exchange your anguish and pain for His healing.

"... and who, at the worst, if he fails,"

How He does this, is through mostly unremarkable people like myself, who also have skin in the game, have experienced a thing or two in life and know without question what it's like, and at the same time offer hope, compassion, understanding and encouragement.

"... at least he fails while daring greatly"

When you look into my eyes, you can see that I get it, know that I get it and then we can have a conversation about how sucky it is, at this moment. Now, this is not to say that I'll leave you there in the bog of despair, sucked into the mire of unforgiveness, bitterness and resentment, rather it is to acknowledge the misery of the moment, the bewilderment of now, and say there is a way through this...

And because you can look into my eyes and see that I know where you're at, you know that I'm telling the truth - same as Jesus when He speaks about stuff He knows - and because of that knowing thing, you find the courage to raise your eyes, to lift your head and to look to The One Unseen Who sees you and knows you, and knows where you're at right now and says "Come to Me, all you who are weary and burdened, and I will give you rest." (Matthew 11: 28 NIV)

> "... so that his place shall never be with those cold and timid souls who knew neither victory nor defeat."

Don't ask me how He does this, all I know is that He does. He is faithful, He is loving, He is kind and He will not fail you.

But...

He will not fail you, He keeps His Promises.

But...

He will not leave you in the middle of your mess, dear heart, it's you who's moved away from Him, or perhaps allowed circumstances to draw you in another direction.

You don't see how He can love you in the midst of this thing. You think that IF He loved you THEN He wouldn't have allowed this thing to happen - that's not love dear one, that's control.

Here is the essence of Free Will. We have Free Will to choose what we want to do - we choose our responses, based on what we have learned and earned and we set the bar for "If you love me, then..." He has already said what Love is, it's there for us in His Word, which if we read it daily, we will find wisdom, and begin to understand His definition of Love.

"Love is patient and kind. Love is not jealous or boastful or proud or rude. It is not irritable, and it keeps no record of being wronged. It does not rejoice about injustice but rejoices whenever truth wins out. Love never gives up, never loses faith, is always hopeful, and endures through every circumstance... Love will last forever!" (1 Corinthians 13 vs 4 - 7, 8c NLT)

This then, is God's definition of Love. This is the standard to which He holds Himself and by which He determines if He has exhibited love towards those whom He loves. Jesus laid down His life in exchange for us. What greater love is there than that?

True, Godly, Pure Love is incredibly difficult to understand - I'm still struggling with it - for it seems to hold two truths together at the same time: this awful thing happened AND I am Loved. It messes with our brains because we have set up what we think it means to love - cue history, experience and what we were taught in our home of origin.

Because of this, we think we know what it means to Love and yet, we forget the *Words* above left for us to think upon.

So, what now?

That's a really good question. I think, and this is my perspective, feel free to use it if it serves you, that we have the opportunity to learn what it means to love in a broken and hurting world.

Love doesn't mean perfect - if it did we would all be automatons without a choice.

Love means imperfect, messy, hurtful, painful and awkward. It also means joy, peace, patience, kindness, goodness, faithfulness, and gentleness and these are bookended with love and self-control. (Galatians 6:22 NLT)

It means we can become mature people, from Romans 5, enduring, resilient to life's quirks, with hope placed firmly in The God who Loves us and allows us the privilege to develop strength of character. It means we grow up and stop behaving like immature children when things don't go our way - you know what I'm saying.

I'm not saying life isn't hard and we shouldn't acknowledge those difficulties, I'm saying we shouldn't wallow in them, complaining and remaining stuck, when God wants us to come to Him.

Jesus said it ever so eloquently and I particularly like how the translation of THE MESSAGE puts it: "Walk with me and work with me - watch how I do it. Learn the unforced rhythms of grace. I won't lay anything heavy or ill-fitting on you." (Matthew 11: 29)

So, now what?

We dare to have conversations. God KNOWS what will heal and what will hurt and though the healing process may be painful, He knows that if you hold on to your bitterness, resentment and pain, it will do you more harm than good; and you DESERVE good!

Acknowledge the pain - don't remain there, though. This is a big one. What happened was awful and in a perfect world, it should never have happened and I'm deeply sorry that it did. Although your experience is uniquely yours, others will have shared something similar. You're not alone.

When you are ready, ask God for an exchange: His beauty for your ashes, His oil of Joy for your mourning, and ask Him to soften and prepare your heart to receive healing.

Then decide what you want to do next.

How would you like to release that pain?

What thing of significance can you do, to say: "This happened, it hurt and I'm doing something that reminds me that I am alive. I have lived through this; I'm not taken out by it and I can be grateful (eventually) for the experience as I now have something of incredible value to share with someone else when they're in need."

"... the credit belongs to the man who is actually **in the arena**, who spends himself in a worthy cause, who at the best, knows, in the end, the triumph of high achievement..."

What is our response?

In my opinion, we have no excuse...

It is awful the things that happen in this life, and no, none of them should happen.

And at the same time they do.

So, what do we do now?

There were times in my life when things looked very bleak. I choose not to be specific about these, as there are other people who were involved and I'd like to respect their privacy.

Suffice to say, I would have sunk into the mires of bitterness and resentment, the bog of eternal despair and the never-ending well of self-pity all in an effort not to deal with the real problem. I needed healing, but I was terrified of it (healing), of finding another reason why I wasn't enough and I was tormented by the things I needed to be healed from. And at the same time, I longed to be healed. I wanted to be better and I wanted to be free from the things that held me bound in the past, I didn't want to react unbecomingly when those memories were triggered, nor hurt those around me and I wanted more than anything else to love wholeheartedly and feel that I was loved in return.

> "... and who, at the worst, if she fails, at least she fails while daring greatly, so that her place shall never be with those cold and timid souls who knew neither victory nor defeat."

Ultimately at the bottom, after languishing there a while, I called out to God as I had many times before, and I said "I can't do this anymore! I'm dying!" I ran towards Him for my life and I put my trust in people who were well-trained to help me through the healing process.

Not that it was easy!

But I found something interesting after the first time or two... I was grieving with hope. There was no more hopelessness. I felt better after each huge ugly crying, snot-offering session with the Therapists and in my journaling time at home.

I began to see progress as I healed. Things that used to bother me now don't. Things I couldn't possibly have done before were now within reach and became manageable as I learned how to navigate - without being crushed by - Imposter Syndrome, the equally cruel twins: *Fear of Success* and *Fear of Failure* and their younger sibling *I'm Not Good Enough-itis*.

A recent diagnosis of ADHD has helped me to understand that I see, interact with and comprehend the world around me in a significantly different manner from neurotypical folk. It's also explained a host of "symptoms" - or strengths used in the wrong place - that I didn't realise were "symptoms," I just thought they were more evidence of my "wrongness."

Now I realise that my hyperfocus on proving everyone right who told me I was wrong could be more profitably used to get my books out into the public arena. Match this with insatiable curiosity, creativity and perpetual mental motion and you have an Author, Coach and Resource Builder with endless ideas.

Focus my boundless energy in the direction of meeting and greeting principals, teachers, parents, and people worldwide and you have the potential for endlessly successful Courageous Conversations which equip people with the skills, tools and techniques that they need in order to be successful in their daily lives, whatever that means for them.

As I said earlier I'm a mostly unremarkable person, and I'd actually prefer to remain under the radar. However, inside of me is a greater WHY than there is fear, a more powerful Purpose to Serve than there is the desire for anonymity and a far more Loving Being Who Empowers me every day to show up to help you.

Ultimately, my experiences have made me all the more determined to educate through Intentional Writing, Courageous Coaching and Explorative Teaching. I do this by engaging with people where they're at through writing intelligent stories, equipping them by using a wide lexicon, empowering them through questions and exploring possibilities to ensure robust well-thought-out decisions from which they can take positive forward action and live well with the results.

"Who, at the worst, if she fails, at least she fails while daring greatly, so that she may never know her place with those cold and timid souls who knew neither victory nor defeat."

I don't know the path you're on, nor the arena of your influence - everyone has one consciously or not. But this I do know: there is HOPE, FAITH that sustains, and there is LOVE from a Creator Who Knows you better than you know yourself.

If you're anything like I was, think about this: You've lived through 100% of your worst days ever, and you're still here, alive in spite of it all. I made a decision to change my attitude and to find 3 things every day that I could be grateful for and I wrote them down. Each night I wrote down 3 things that I was grateful for, no two days were allowed to be the same things that I was grateful for, and in time, I found that I no longer made a conscious decision to find things, I simply found them unconsciously.

Including when the full bottle of milk slipped from my hands and smashed on the floor and I didn't have the budget for another one that week. I was grateful that I had the opportunity to be grateful for the next bottle of milk and grateful for the opportunity to wash my floor and very grateful I had had milk in the first place and to know the loss of that milk.

Be blessed dear heart, be courageous, but most of all LIVE, because to live would be
    "...an awfully big adventure." ~Peter Pan[8]

---

[8] Barrie, J.M. (1911). *Peter and Wendy 1st US Edition*. (Released later as Peter Pan). New York, NY. Charles Scribner's Sons.

Granny Mac
AUTHOR & SPEAKER

Wife, Author, Curious Explorer, ADHD and Mental Health Courageous Conversations Coach

About the Author

Sarah McCall, through her alter ego Granny Mac, shares skills, tools and wisdom that she has earned and learned in her decades-long walk towards Mental Health Resilience, and Personal Development.

"When you work with me, we unlock frustration, overwhelm & distress to Empower, Equip & Enable you to make well-thought-out Decisions, that withstand rigorous peer review and find the confident, calm & hopeful you, you always knew was hidden inside."

Her hope is that you begin to view your experiences through the lenses of gratitude, thankfulness and hope.

Granny Mac and her Sweet Man live in rural New Zealand, where they enjoy walks along country roads with their adventurous cat, Sofia.

FIND ME
https://www.facebook.com/GrannyMacNZ
https://www.grannymac.co.nz
grannymacnz@gmail.com

The Artist Haven

While I speak about the call to persevere in our creative calling, my co-author, Susan is a great example of this. Have you ever wondered what it would look like to follow your purpose all the way to owning your own studio and helping other artists and creatives thrive? Susan shares her story of growing in her passion to help others blossom in their creative endeavours.

Dedication

I would like to dedicate this story to my wonderful children, their partners and my grandchildren, who all possess their own unique and quirky creative talents. Also, to the many students I have taught. Being part of your lives has enriched me in all that I am and all that I do. Believe in yourself and embrace your talents; water the seeds and keep growing. You are all very special. Remember... be you, because everyone else is taken!

~Susan

Soul Art

Susan Curtin
Artist & Teacher of Art &
Creative Writing

NSW, Australia

"Whether you succeed or not is irrelevant,
there is no such thing.
Making your unknown known is the important thing."
~ Georgia O'Keeffe[9]

My Artistic Journey

For as long as I can remember, I have wanted to be an artist. However, the doors have not always been open and the desire to be a female artist in the 1970s was not often met with applause. Then, as a sixteen year old, I was accepted into an art school based on my artistic merit *but* there were rules! I had to be 18! My young self-believed that if my art was good enough, then age should not matter! School was not my favourite place unless I was in the art room or playing sports, so I left, probably in rebellion to the rule that I must be 18 to enter art school.

Looking back, I did enjoy learning and was a sponge in the classroom, soaking up all that was taught and pondering nature, framed by science and geography lessons. As a child, I devoured books and reread all the children's books in our local town

---

[9] "Georgia O'Keefe." 100 Quotes on Art & Creativity. Retrieved from: https://masterpiecesociety.com/100-quotes-art-creativity/

library a few times before moving on to the adult section. Art books, however, were not plentiful in those days and with no such thing as the internet, I had to make do with encyclopedias to read about the art masters.

English was also a subject which holds strong memories and my love for the written word has stayed with me. Despite doing very well in school, I never studied, even for tests, and wanted more outside of school. Too impatient to complete another two years of schooling, I began a career in the world of finance. My yearning to paint though, never left me.

Fast forward to marriage and two children... I began painting again. Much to my surprise, I entered the university to become a teacher. This was never part of my early plan but it happened, and I have never looked back. Life held different priorities and responsibilities at that time. My children were my number one priority. Teaching was a huge responsibility and also consumed much of my time, leaving no room for painting. However, I spent decades collecting and reading art books; filling the filing cabinets in my brain with everything I could about my favourite artists, art materials, art practices and processes.

Fast forward again to my retirement... and my reward... I was able to paint again. Finally. Repressing this urge has been difficult and my hope is that women artists will find the path much easier for them today. After opening a gallery and working studio, I now paint and teach, combining two of my loves.

Getting back to nature has also been an important part of my transition to artist. The love of nature and the art *in* nature has been with me all my life. Being immersed in nature dominates my earliest memories and provides an endless supply of inspiration for my art practice. Exploring elements in coastal fringes, such as estuaries, mangroves, rock pools and even the behaviour of soldier crabs and octopi offers so much creative material. A fascination in the variation in water patterns and colours, markings on rock platforms and cliff faces, seaweed, spiral shells and the beautiful forms of cowries and murexes offer endless possibilities for the artist.

"To the artist there is never anything ugly in nature."
~Auguste Rodin[10]

Curiosity has ensured that I find wonder and awe in the minutiae; not just the outer appearance but the inner workings of all things. It is in our observation of the natural world that we find perfection; the golden ratio, division of cells and growth cycles such as the rings inside trees... it is all there for us to explore and replicate in our imperfect artwork, representing the beauty surrounding us as best we can.

*The poet, **Henry Wadsworth Longfellow**, said it best with:*
Nature is a revelation of God; Art a revelation of man.[11]

The pursuit of perfection is always there for the artist but finding it is another story. Instead, the best we can hope for and attain is the joy that can be felt in this pursuit, the endless process of play, exploration, experimentation and discovery. Since we cannot create as God, we can only humanise the experience of creation in our artwork.

---

[10] Neuendorf, H. (2016). 10 Inspiring Quotes by Auguste Rodin on his 176th Birthday. Artnet News. Retrieved from: https://news.artnet.com/art-world/auguste-rodin-birthday-quotes-745238
[11] AZ Quotes. (n.d.) Quotes. Retrieved from: https://www.azquotes.com/quote/535178

Every artist dips his brush into his own soul, and
paints his own nature into his pictures.
~ Henry Ward Beecher[12]

Searching for our own creative language can reveal a myriad of pathways. The renown singer and songwriter, Jim Morrison said, *"There are things known and things unknown and in between are the doors."*

Why do I paint? It's all about the doors!

I am addicted to everything "art." I *have* to paint. I *need* to paint. It is an obsession, a compulsion. I don't have to hold it back anymore. The creative door has been opened and there are many more ahead.

To create, is to immerse myself into that magic cocoon that embraces me when I focus, shutting out everything else around me. Just my art and I. Being creative anchors my soul. It provides peace and tranquility.

"Art washes away from the soul the dust of everyday life."
~ Pablo Picasso[13]

I am also passionate about teaching and sharing the joy that comes from being creative. There is so much risk taking involved in being creative.

As adults we tend to think that everything we do should be perfect; acceptable to ourselves and others. We want others

---

[12] "Henry Ward Beecher." 100 Quotes on Art & Creativity. Retrieved from: https://masterpiecesociety.com/100-quotes-art-creativity/
[13] "Pablo Picasso" 100 Quotes on Art & Creativity. Retrieved from: https://masterpiecesociety.com/100-quotes-art-creativity/

to love what we do or we can be left feeling that we are a failure. We generally care about what people think. However, thoughts such as these can sabotage our true creative potential by preventing us from persisting and growing our unique innate talents. No wonder Oscar Wilde[14] said, "Be yourself, everyone else is already taken.'

Create art for yourself first and foremost. Enjoy the process. Play. Have fun!

> *"Every child is an artist. The problem is how to*
> *remain an artist once we grow up."*
> *~ Pablo Picasso[15]*

Find the child within; that uninhibited child who does not care about the end result. Be loose and free like you once were. Observe a child's painting with no rules. Be that child. There is so much freedom in creating an artwork using this carefree approach. Sure, there are rules, but rules were meant to be broken. Just as a poet breaks rules, so does the artist. Rules in art can confine artistic expression and tighten the results. However, knowing the rules is necessary in order to break them; to find true artistic freedom. *But...* rules can be learnt through the process of play, exploration and discovery. Immersing yourself in a supportive artistic group, painting with a friend and learning together, feeling safe and encouraged, are the

---

[14] Forbes.comLLC. (2015). Forbes Quotes: Thoughts on the Business of Life. Retrieved from:
https://www.forbes.com/quotes/11441/#:~:text=Be%20yourself%3B%20everyone%20e lse%20is,Oscar%20Wilde%20%2D%20Forbes%20Quotes
[15] Martelle, A. (2023). Picasso and the Art of Children: Let Textiles Talk Log #7. Retrieved from: https://stedelijkstudies.com/picasso-and-the-art-of-children/#:~:text=Pablo%20Picasso%20famously%20said%3A,artist%20once%20we%20 grow%20up.%E2%80%9D

ingredients for progress, confidence and positive self-esteem as you find your true creative expression.

Edward Hopper once said, "If I could say it in words there would be no reason to paint." Art is visual poetry, eliminating words and sentences and just allowing the visuals to speak for itself.[16]

When I was a sign language interpreter, the movement of my arms and hands was like painting with two hands; painting a visual language that replaces the common language of written symbols and graphemes that are spoken. Sign language can say so much more than spoken words, just like a painting. An artwork can talk to us through silent visuals. An exchange of thoughts and conversation can provoke internal self-talk. Sometimes the message is loud and clear. Sometimes it is not. Emotions may be evoked. Love and admiration can wash over us. A wrenching or struggle may ensue. Art will not always make you "feel good" but you *will* feel. You will respond; anywhere from dismissive to elation and all the positive and negative in between.

"Art should comfort the disturbed and disturb the comfortable."
~ Cesar Cruz[17]

Do I always have to know what my artwork will look like before I start? No, unless of course I am painting a commission such as a portrait. The process of making expressive, fluid art, is in itself,

---

[16] "Edward Hopper." 100 Quotes on Art & Creativity. Retrieved from: https://masterpiecesociety.com/100-quotes-art-creativity/
[17] GoodReads. (2023). Quotable Quote. Retrieved from: https://www.goodreads.com/quotes/622456-art-should-comfort-the-disturbed-and-disturb-the-comfortable

medicine for the heart, mind and soul. Not knowing where a painting is going is like unwrapping layers on a pass-the-parcel. Trusting the process and looking forward to the surprise at the end is exciting! Enjoy the layers, the pulling and pushing of form, tone and line.

So how do you start a painting when you don't know what you are going to do? I have a routine where I take a large watercolour brush, laden with water, and smack it onto a white piece of paper. Next, I choose a coloured ink and just place one or two drops into the water splash. The ink manages to find all those fine water lines on the edges, creating an image that will inspire ideas that can then be explored. Settling for only one medium can often prevent thorough exploration, so I introduce a water soluble crayon from my favourite Caran d'ache Neocolour II set. Play is important. And so on and on it goes, adding and taking away, using gel pens, watercolour, gouache and at times, collage. If I hit a point where I do not know how to finish it, the painting is simply put to one side and a new one started.

"Creativity takes courage."
~ Henri Matisse[18]

So take a risk. Be brave. Put a mark on the page, bend it, stretch it, tighten it, reduce, enlarge, narrow it, widen it, make it wavy, scratch it. Authentic learning through *doing* will always result in meaningful outcomes.

---

[18] "Henri Matisse." 100 Quotes on Art & Creativity. Retrieved from: https://masterpiecesociety.com/100-quotes-art-creativity/

"An artist never really finishes his work;
he merely abandons it."
~ Paul Valéry[19]

Paintings do not have to be finished in one day. Feel free to put it aside. Revisit it and wait for it to speak to you, calling you to the next layer. Do not force it. Let it happen naturally. Paintings that are not fully resolved will sometimes find their way into other paintings as collage. Recycling unfinished artworks can provide the pieces that make other artworks come to life when they have nowhere else to go. Nothing is wasted. Recognise the value in recycling and you will keep surprising yourself with fresh ideas for your arts practice.

Creating in this way results in challenges that need to be resolved. Embrace the challenges and learn from them. Enjoy the process, for art is indeed a process that can be enjoyed. Be in the moment and your cares will drift away as you immerse yourself and play. Vincent van Gogh said it so well with: *"The emotions are sometimes so strong that I work without knowing it. The strokes come like speech*[20]*."* And Twyla Tharp tells us that, *"Art is the only way to run away without leaving home*[21]*."*

Art is for Everyone

It is my belief that art should be accessible to everyone, regardless of their perceived ability or disability. Any attempt at art-making is an ability. An ability that belongs to the individual,

[19] "Paul Valéry." 100 Quotes on Art & Creativity. Retrieved from: https://masterpiecesociety.com/100-quotes-art-creativity/
[20] Jerry's Artarama. (n.d.). Art Quotes & Famous Artists Quotes. Retrieved from: https://www.jerrysartarama.com/blog/famous-artist-quotes/
[21] "Twyla Tharp." 100 Quotes on Art & Creativity. Retrieved from: https://masterpiecesociety.com/100-quotes-art-creativity/

the art maker. It is our differences that make the art world so fascinating, complex to understand at times *and* controversial. Everyone possesses the ability to make something original that is also of value to someone else.

So how do I go about teaching art? It's all about the unique individual in front of me. I believe in the ability of my students, whether they are experienced or not. I believe that reciprocal teaching and learning happens when we gather to create. Everyone has a forte, a niche in art and I am passionate about helping my students find their unique creative self. Facilitating transformations in students about the way they approach their art practice and their own self-belief is essential.

Teaching people *how* to think rather than *what* to think is important to me. How do you plant seeds for creativity, whether it be writing, painting, sculpting or other creative practices? Be in touch with your feelings. Our five senses are extremely important in the creative process. One of my students came to my creative writing class with a button. Not just any button. It belonged to her dad. This button had been to the Second World War and home again. It had faced death and depravity, been in the trenches, covered in mud, held tears and fears. This button survived the unimaginable and then... was lost for 70 years. When visiting her childhood hometown, Trish dared to knock on the door of her family's old farmhouse. The current owners shared their renovation stories with her. Then, they mentioned the recent discovery of a button in the old farm shed out the back. Found buried in the earthen floor, they recognised that it was a military button and became intrigued about its origins and how it got there.

Upon being handed the button, the memories swept over Trish and she knew she had to write about it. What memories did it carry? What smells did it evoke? The sounds, feelings and sights came back to her, just by holding this button. Writing became Trish's art form. There were stories that had to be told and they poured from her.

One day, Samantha walked into my studio with a carer and a guide dog. Now this is a true tale of bravery and a creative voice that would not be silenced. I was beyond thrilled that Samantha expressed a creative desire and had no intention of letting her sight impairment stop her. And so our journey began...

The creation of 3D sculptures has opened up Samantha's art practice, using items that are meaningful to her to weave her stories. It is all about the texture and form. The sensitivity of her fingertips allows her to create clay pieces and impressions that hold the texture and form that represent her world. Weaving natural fibres through pieces of wood, incorporating shells and driftwood with familiar connections of community and friendship, Samantha creates unique pieces that must be touched and explored as you are taken into her world. Her pieces are for the sighted and the blind. There are no limits to what Samantha can achieve. With hands to see and feel her way, every opportunity is seized and her creative talent continues to grow today. Recently, Samantha bought a Dremel tool set and cannot wait to start using it. Nothing is impossible!

The famed artist, Georgia O'Keeffe said, *"To create one's own world takes courage,*[22]*"* and Samantha has this in spades!

If we take Edgar Degas literally, "Art is not what you see but what you make others see[23]," Samantha has managed to open a whole new world, not just for herself, but for others. The inspiration she exudes is infectious. Visitors to my studio and gallery are amazed to watch her working. Art is not always about what you see but what you feel, physically and emotionally.

Another student I teach who has Parkinson's Disease, is encouraged to let their shaking hands create their own painting language. The results are amazing! If we do not fight our perceived limitations and instead embrace them, allowing them into our artwork, the results are truly unique and an authentic reflection of ourselves at that time.

Teaching students with special needs continues to be an enriching experience. Seeing the transformation in students is cause for celebration... and there are many!

When I teach, no one makes mistakes; we create learning opportunities. No one fails because we are supporting one another in an inclusive creative environment where we are all growing and developing as individuals. The only limitations we have are those we place on ourselves.

---

[22] "Georgia O'Keeffe." 100 Quotes on Art & Creativity. Retrieved from: https://masterpiecesociety.com/100-quotes-art-creativity/
[23] "Edgar Degas." 100 Quotes on Art & Creativity. Retrieved from: https://masterpiecesociety.com/100-quotes-art-creativity/

"If I were called upon to define briefly the word Art,
I should call it the reproduction of what the
senses perceive in nature,
seen through the veil of the soul."
~ Paul Cezanne[24]

For anyone who would like to explore their creative side, I want to tell you to trust yourself and believe you are already creative. Do not listen to voices that may say you are not creative or cannot do it! I strongly believe that we are all meant to be creative. Do not measure yourself with anyone else or put any expectations on your artwork. Just play. Do it for you! Let your authentic self-shine. You are a unique individual and as you paint and create, no-one will do it the same way as you.

Susan Curtin

"Abandoned Beauty"

---

[24] AZ Quotes. Quotable Quote. Retrieved from:
https://www.azquotes.com/author/2665-
Paul_Cezanne/tag/art#:~:text=If%20I%20were%20called%20upon,the%20veil%20of%20
the%20soul.

"Out of the Ashes" refers to my chapter because it is about recovery, renewal, and regeneration after the bushfires. It's about coming together and represents the strength of the community to rally and rebuild homes and reestablish farms and livestock numbers to grow and heal. This is what creative art does for us, too.

"Fragile Contemplation"

About the Author

Susan Curtin is an artist, teacher, and owner of The Art Hub - Studio & Gallery in Nowra, South Coast NSW Australia. As an artist, following her own path and painting for herself is an important aspect of her art practice. This ensures that her emotional wellbeing benefits from the mindfulness and peace that comes with painting. Susan is equally determined that the students she teaches also benefit from the therapeutic wellbeing that springs from creative practices. As a teacher, her mission is to support others in finding their innate talents and unique, authentic artistic language. Difference and diversity in art is to be embraced and celebrated, regardless of a students' background or experience. Art truly *is* for everyone.

FIND ME:

Facebook: https://www.facebook.com/susancurtinart
and https://www.facebook.com/TheArtHubNOWRA
Instagram: https://www.instagram.com/dragonfly77w/
Email: thearthub45@gmail.com

The Artist Haven

Despite all the odds stacked against her, Samantha's story is one of remarkable courage and determination. Being a blind artist in the creative area of visual arts would seem to be a complete contradiction or oxymoron. However, Samantha has an important life lesson for us all. She has turned her disability into an ability. Your perception of art will be forever challenged as Samantha explains how she creates artworks that she will never see, only feel. Using her hands as her eyes, Samantha's story will both move and inspire you.

Dedication

I would like to dedicate this chapter to Andrew, for putting a power tool in my hand and telling me to go for it. And to Susan Curtin, for creating The Art Hub, a haven for the creative, and for believing I can do anything.
-Samantha

Hands That See Beauty

Samantha Ogilvie
Mixed Media Artist, Designer

Shoalhaven NSW, Australia

If you cannot imagine it you cannot have it.
~Toni Morrison[25]

I picked up my stylus and tapped into my creativity. From as early as I can remember, I've been told that I have a fantastic imagination. I could play by myself for hours.

At age four, I was diagnosed with cancer; a fatal tumour behind my right eye, my ethmoid sinuses, and a centimeter along my pituitary stalk. I spent a large proportion of the next few years in hospitals, either having procedures, tests, or waiting for appointments, etc. to be over and done with. My sister Rebekah had the misfortune of having to be dragged along. It was boring and frustrating for both of us. I started making up stories to entertain us. When I look back on those times, I think those stories helped keep the fear away for both of us too. My creativity has remained an integral part of my life.

It wasn't just stories that I created. I also loved to play with clay. There is a rather telling photo of me around five years of age, covered in chicken pox, sitting at my mother's pottery

---

[25] LiteraryArts.com (n.d.) Toni Morrison, March 19, 1992. Portland, Oregon. Retrieved from: https://literary-arts.org/archive/toni-morrison/

wheel. I do not remember that photo being taken, but I do remember all the enjoyment I got out of creating.

In primary school, I began to write poetry as well as stories. I also wrote plays that my friends and I would perform in front of our class. For a few months in year six, I took acting classes. I loved it. I loved being able to become someone else for a brief time. It helped me cope with the ongoing medical appointments with what I saw back then, as the ongoing betrayal of my body. I hated my body; it was my enemy. Constantly failing me when I needed it to be strong. Being able to lose myself in a character, a story, I forget about the day-to-day, the fact that I was blind, was magic. I loved it, unfortunately, it didn't last long.

When my cancer was diagnosed and we learned that I was going blind, this wasn't a time for giving up or giving in. My mother told me that cancer could be beaten, and of course, it was. She also told me that "being blind didn't mean I couldn't do things. It just meant that we might have to go about some things in different ways."

I wouldn't be here now, writing this chapter if my mother hadn't instilled this mantra in me. People had always noticed that my right eye looked different from my left. It sat out a little and was predominately turned in towards my nose. The lower lid had dropped and the white of the eye was scarred red. Strangers would ask what was wrong with my eye.

It annoyed me that these people were focusing on the ugly part of my body, for it was ugly to me. I didn't like people only seeing that negative part of me. Sometimes kids wouldn't want to play with me because of my eye. That didn't upset me, it just frustrated me. It only became a serious issue when I started high school.

It was the first week of year seven. I was already feeling overwhelmed by everything. I was catching public transport for the first time on my own and learning to negotiate the ocean of teenagers that had swelled from my primary school puddle. I already felt small and insignificant, like I was being swept along by a current determined to drown me. And then I went to my first social science class.

I hadn't come to high school on my own. Most of the kids in my year six class had come to the same high school. It was my friends from that group that kept me anchored in those first few days. That changed when the social science teacher arrived and announced: "You have two minutes to move to whichever seat you would like, after those two minutes, you will have to sit there for the rest of the year." I didn't move. Why would I? All my friends were sitting around me. What I didn't expect was that all of my friends got up as one and moved to a different part of the room. There was nothing said, nothing done to warn me. They just got up and left me surrounded by empty chairs. They never spoke to me again, except to tease and taunt me.

They weren't the only ones to tease and bully me. A considerable proportion of kids saw me as the perfect target. It was almost too easy to target blind, doggy-eye, and even better, someone who often wet themselves. It would be nearly twenty years before we learned that one of my chemo drugs had affected my bladder, causing incontinence and sharp intense pains in my abdomen. Not to mention, this was long before reliable and appropriate aids for incontinence became available.

All of this contributed to my need to be invisible to the bullies. I wouldn't speak in class if not called on. I even dumbed myself down, writing assignments that would get me a pass, but nothing higher. I became silent and fearful, always swallowing down my thoughts and feelings. This is how I navigated high school.

The only class I let myself be truly myself, was art.

I still can't explain it. It just didn't occur to me to hold back in my art classes. I embraced my creativity. I unfolded, stretching and extending to take myself back.

It was my therapy and my voice. What I could never have put into words or action in the rest of my life, I turned into sculptors and pastel creations. Never fearing the consequences. Not caring what the other students would do or say. In my art, I could be brave. Even in year eight, when the new art teacher, Mrs. Arbor, chose to ignore me, believing that an art class was no place for a blind person, I didn't run and hide.

I didn't run to the head teacher or the principal asking to be changed into a different elective. I showed up to class, took my seat, and waited. There was no way I was going to give in first. Mrs. Arbor gave in first, choosing to leave the school, rather than teaching me. Her replacement was the polar opposite. I'm sure this contributed to my confidence in my art.

And I still wrote. Self-obsessed poetry and fantasy stories. The poetry was the purging of the negativity from school. The fantasy was an escape from my life for a time. Just like the stories I used to tell my sister when we were younger through all those hours and hours of hospital visits.

I used to destroy the poetry and stories. I thought it was because I didn't like it, that it wasn't worth keeping. And yes, I did believe this. What I know now though, was that it was therapy, a cleansing. It was only when I saw *Dead Poet's Society* that I stopped destroying my work.

"Cut you and you'll bleed poetry" is a statement made to me by a friend when we were chatting one day. And this statement made me realise how integral to my life poetry is. I don't see my poetry as therapy anymore but a place where I can always be honest with myself.

My creativity has always nourished me. It's kept me balanced, whether it has simply given me the opportunity to drain all the negativity that's built up in my body and mind, or because I have something to say, it's always there. Pieces of my work have been published in various writing journals, but most are no longer in circulation anymore.

If I go for a period of time, anything over three or four days without creating, my body and mind become affected. It's like my blood is too full, too heavy. And the poison that results from this glut of blood, starts to tease and manipulate my mind. I become anxious, and depressed and can not cope with the general day-to-day world.

Many people have helped me expand and learn more about my creative self and what I'm capable of achieving. My mum and members of my family, teachers at the university, a beautiful friend and mentor, Asheel Jedrzejak; and my writing group at the Art Hub in the Shoalhaven that I have been a member for one year. I have found The Art Hub to be my Oasis where I connect with like-minded creatives who uplift me and encourage me on my journey of life.

I've always been brave in my creative life and refused to accept limitations or hurdles. This has become even more apparent since I became a part of the Art Hub family here in Nowra. My work has changed and grown exponentially, going from 2 to 3 dimensional, seemingly overnight. My current works are sculptures in wood, clay, shells, and other jewels found in nature. All are woven and stitched together to tell stories and perspectives I've not shared before.

In April 2023, I entered one of these sculptures into the Shoalhaven Mental Health Fellowship Prize. I was just excited that my work would hang in the regional gallery. So I was completely amazed and overwhelmed when my piece, *See Web*, won third prize.

This is how I expressed myself through my art piece, *See Web*: "My world is full of texture and sound. *See Web* reflects my inner and outer worlds. The differing threads and woven textures represent tides of emotions, good and bad, different paths and connections with people and places. The clay impressions caught in the web are my refuge. Because of my eyes, I think others judge me as ugly. This perception and the trials this presents creates the irritation felt on the clay surface. However, I can subvert this, and with my hands, only see the beauty in this texture. My hands are my eyes. The texture is the fabric of my existence."

Samantha Ogilvie

Samantha Ogilvie

"The Art Hub"
Samantha creating in her safe haven.

About the Author

Samantha Ogilvie is an artist. Her passion for art has taken her to many places in life. She loves poetry and her dog, getting amongst other artists, and learning new ways to create and learn new skills. Samantha's art makes her brave and has taught her to believe anything is possible within her reach. Samantha loves being able to share this philosophy with others and knowing that she does this daily at The Art Hub, just by being there and creating and allowing other adults and children to observe her work, its creation and to ask her any questions. The giving back is just as important as her creativity. She hopes her words here will inspire you to reach for the stars, they are waiting for you.

FIND ME:

Facebook: Dot the Eyes by Samantha Ogilvie blog
https://www.facebook.com/profile.php?id=100066401210089
Instagram @ https://www.instagram.com/dot_the_eyes/

The Artist Haven

I am indeed brave when it comes to my art. Sometimes being brave looks like doing the next right thing, no matter what. Angie, a fellow artist shares this experience as she learned how to take the next small step to elevate her creativity and receive inspiration in a fresh way.

Dedication

I dedicate this work to my husband Markus and my children Jenny and André. They have been with me through ups and downs and this little family is a real home for me. I also dedicate this work to my Father God who has carried me so many times and I am very grateful to see how He has bound us closely together.
~Angie

I Am Not the Abandoned One
But the Beloved One!

Angela Günther
Artist

Ludwigsburg, Germany

Therefore, if anyone is united with the Messiah,
he is a new creation the old has passed;
look, what has come is fresh and new.
1 Corinthians 5:17 (JNT)

My Childhood

I was always this child who looked at nature with eyes full of wonder. I picked flowers and looked at them very closely. I examined the colours, the shapes and all the other details.

I spent hours and hours on the beach and felt engrossed staring and hearing as waves made splashes against the rocks. I marveled at the tall, rocky and green mountains when we went on vacations. I could never understand how people around me did not seem to notice or appreciate the beauty of creation

I remember my father practicing painting with me. I loved it. He made it look really easy. I remember how he would add scribbles to the letters of the alphabet and make little animals. I was totally a daddy's girl.

At the tender age of six, my parents were divorced and this caused so much disruption to my life. My father, unfortunately, was an alcoholic and became aggressive. That was the last straw for my mother. We moved to another city and that's where my mother met my stepfather.

That time was very difficult for me. I had to leave my beloved great grandmother, my friends, and of course my dad. My great-grandmother was the only friend I had. We always had a good time together. I remember how she would laugh every time I said I wanted to paint when she asked me what I wanted to do.

I retreated into my own little shell after those sad and unfortunate events. A very dark time in my life happened when I was seven years old. Unbeknownst to us, my stepfather had abusive tendencies and I became the object of his abuse. I was lonely from leaving the life I used to know, and he took advantage of that. I had very conflicting emotions because he had been very kind to me. He took me hiking, swimming, and fishing. I was so confused and I didn't know what I was supposed to feel. I completely shut down from then on. I had sleepless nights. I became so fearful not just of my stepfather but of people in general. I felt so much shame. I felt that I did something wrong. I had this feeling I can't explain.

This experience affected my school performance. I had difficulty concentrating. It was so overwhelming and I felt that my life was going down the drain. What kept me going were my weekend trips to my old hometown. I got to spend time with my great-grandmother, my girlfriends, and especially my father. Those weekend trips went on for a few years. It felt so liberating to be away from the presence of my stepfather. My dad also remarried and had three children with his new wife. I remember their nice house with a garden. My half-siblings had their own rooms! I would have liked that, but I was merely a guest in their house.

Things were going smoothly during my weekend visits with my dad and his new family until one day, I learned that his new wife wanted me to stop visiting. I could not describe the pain I felt when my dad told me that he would not pick me up anymore. To add insult to injury, he wanted me to understand what his new wife wanted to happen. Though he assured me that he would visit me some time, it didn't make me feel any better. I still have the picture in my head of how I stood on the street waiting for him for hours. What was there to understand? He didn't want me around! How could I bear that pain?

I became a very "shy loner" in school because of all that happened to me. I became an introvert. I didn't want to be around people. I often spaced out and looked blankly in the school yard through the window of the classroom. My teachers encouraged my mom to bring me to see a psychologist because of the disturbing behavior they were observing. I also started locking myself in my bedroom. Somehow I wanted to feel I was protecting myself. I developed some allergies and started scratching my body until my skin bled. I was in terrible shape.

Growing Pains into Adulthood.

I wanted to escape my home life so when I met my first husband at age eighteen, I didn't think twice and moved in with him. I put all my energy and attention on sports to distract myself. I was successful in playing sports and it somehow boosted my self-confidence. Though I was feeling confident about myself, I still had panic attacks around people. I felt like so many pairs of eyes were looking at me with hate and disgust when I stroll around big shopping malls.

My boyfriend and I got married when I was twenty-one and we were blessed with two children soon after. Life was very busy raising my children and I didn't do much creative work for many years. I was content and happy painting the walls of our apartment every few months.

Despite the seemingly good things that were happening in my life, I found myself struggling with symptoms of childhood abuse. I thought I already overcame it somehow. Little did I know, it was still creeping into the details of my life. There was a sense of rejection and self-loathing inside of me. I hid behind a good layer of makeup to mask all the pain, shame, weakness, and vulnerability. I wanted to appear like this invincible woman.

My Identity Transformed as I Encountered Love.

One day, my mum invited me to attend a church service with her. I politely turned her down, but that didn't keep her from trying. I would have kept turning her down had I not found my marriage in a desperate situation. My husband became an alcoholic and spent most of his time partying. Flashbacks of my childhood experiences with my own father came back to me. I felt lonely as my husband became indifferent towards me. In my despair, I decided to go to church with my mum as I felt trapped in my marriage raising my children and did not want to repeat what I had experienced in my life.

My life took a 180-degree turn when I watched a healing service video of Benny Hinn that my mum gave me. People who were in wheelchairs were standing and walking for the first time in years. I saw many miracles: the blind receiving their sight and the deaf their hearing. Watching this made a huge impact on my life! I broke down and wept before the presence of the Lord. One thing was immediately clear to me that day: there is a merciful God who loves me, who takes an interest in my life, and who is not indifferent to people. The following Sunday, I willingly went with my mum to church and gave my life to Jesus. I had an unexplainable sense of peace, joy and hope. I knew that my life was about to change.

I became so hungry for God. It was insatiable that I had to attend every church service and conference. I asked every God-fearing person I met about the power of Jesus. I was thirsty to receive as much as I could from the Lord! I said to Him, "Lord, I want all that You have prepared for me, I want to fulfill my purpose here on earth." Inwardly, I knew immediately that this would come with a price.

Following my encounter with the Lord, I married my current husband. Our marriage had not been smooth because of our past, and a portion of that was because I had been married before. We went through valleys and deserts together while God was healing me from the previous marriage. Despite all that, God had not stopped working in my life. He has never left me as he has poured his loving power into me which has brought much healing and forgiveness to my life.

New Artistic Beginning: Overcoming by Grace.

My desire to paint came alive again! God's healing touch led me to go back to what I love the most: painting. A brand new world opened up to me as I held my brush and started attending a course on watercolour painting. I had so much fun! I could not stop myself from painting and I became unaware of how much time had passed! I kept painting until the wee hours of the night. It didn't take long until I started using blank canvases and acrylic paints. God had never stopped working in my life. He had uncovered aching wounds and healed them all one by one. In every brush stroke I made on a blank canvas, there was also the blood of Christ covering all the guilt, shame, pain, anger, and confusion until my heart and mind were white as snow.

This new journey was not a smooth ride. I encountered dead ends not knowing what to paint, and I found myself staring on a blank canvas with no ideas. I could have continued painting from existing pictures, but I felt that I could do more. I felt like there was something inside me waiting to be born, but it could not get out. I put my passion for painting on a shelf one more time out of frustration. I hit rock bottom once again.

The rejection and betrayal I experienced from people I considered brothers and sisters in the faith did not help at all. I fell right back into depression. Getting up in the morning became a painful ordeal. On top of that, I developed an autoimmune disease, I presumed because of all the trauma I have experienced over the years. I felt like I was in a deep, dark hole and I could not get out. I cried to the Lord for help and He did not fail me. He gave me the grace to get back on my feet and start worshiping. Slowly, I found the strength to pick up my brushes and start painting. I didn't know what to paint so I just painted a very colorful heart. I was surprised that it turned out to be a beautiful artwork. I kept making heart paintings and gave them away. People were blessed by my artwork.

Someone once told me that my paintings would not just be beautiful pieces but would tell heavenly stories. It was hard for me to believe those words, but I still tried. I prayed and soaked in the presence of the Lord. I waited for inspiration from the Lord so I could paint those pictures of heaven, but it never came. My heart was pained that I couldn't express my creativity through my painting.

I finally had a revelation from the Lord after spending hours seeking Him and being in His presence! God is the creator and He has called me to create! I didn't have to paint pictures of heaven because whatever I created was God-inspired and was a reflection of God's glory. Whatever I create will touch people's lives because the ideas were flowing from the source of all life; God Himself!

A New Freedom in My Creativity

Knowing that my identity is in Christ was very liberating! This gave me the courage to paint again. I set up a large blank canvas, unpacked my paint and picked up a palette knife. I had no plan, but I just had this deep desire to create. I made my very first abstract painting that night and I was ecstatic! Joy rose up from within me and I had a breakthrough! The need to create a perfect piece was gone! I felt free to be who I am and allow the gift that God gave to flow through me. I felt that I received the greatest gift anyone could ever receive; His resurrection power living and working in and through me. I now understood that God made each one of us in a very special and unique way and He wants us to enjoy that freedom! We don't have to compare ourselves with others. Instead, let us discover the gifts and talents that God has so generously blessed us with and use them for His glory.

I started producing multiple paintings. I often used my spatula technique for the background of my pieces and painted over them. I had so much fun allowing the Lord to guide me with every painting. The Holy Spirit would often lead me to use certain colors not knowing how the painting will end up looking afterwards. The Lord kept using my paintings to personally minister to me. The themes were often what God was teaching me at that moment. The paintings may be about animals or nature, but they all reflected "life" as God is the "giver and keeper of life."

My passion is to bring a piece of heaven to earth with each painting. The technique is of less importance because what really mattered was bringing heaven to earth. What is significant was to allow God to minister healing through my paintings.

Thank you Lord for Colours

Colours touch the deepest parts of our souls just as music does. I remember how I was genuinely touched by the work of an artist in a church service. He was invited to do a live painting. With the Holy Spirit as his guide, he started painting and I felt as if God was healing me as he put colours on a blank canvas. I melted in the presence of the Lord and was overwhelmed by his healing love.

Because of my awareness of the effect of colours on the human soul, I kept using strong colours in my work. I started experimenting with various techniques and mediums.

Some days were more difficult than others. I experienced pain in my hands, fingers, shoulder and back because of rheumatoid arthritis. It used to throw me off track with my painting, but not anymore. I persisted and kept painting because I found so much joy and life in it. I believe that our good God who has carried me through all these years will make healing to manifest in my physical body.

As I am writing this, I am finishing a painting. Oh how I love to bask in the flow of the Holy Spirit and allow him to bring heaven to earth through every piece of artwork I create. What I do now was once just a dream, but God made it real, as real as His abounding love. I have gone through peaks and valleys in my life but allow me to encourage everyone to trust the Lord who made the Heavens and the earth. He will see you through the seasons. Allow His glory to manifest in your life. Have fun discovering the gifts and talents He has deposited in your life and continue to be amazed at how He can use you. There is so much more you **can do for the Lord!**

Angela Gunther

"Orchids" - From ashes comes beauty. The Lord uses
even our wounds and brokenness to bring
forth beauty and glory.

"Dream Big" - Even as a child I loved to dream and I
marveled at the beauty of creation.
Then came years in which at some point the dreams had
died, because the world was evil to me. But then God
came and said ...start dreaming again, dream big.
(acrylic mixed media and palette knife technique on canvas}

About the Author

Angela Günther is a housewife, mother of two children, and an
artist., She has served in the pastoral care ministry for inner
healing for years, she was a house group leader and a worship
leader. This is still her passion, as well as her art. Angela's vision

is to see God healing people's spirit, soul and body through music and art.

FIND ME:

Instagram: https://www.instagram.com/angie_g_life_art/
Email: angiels-life-art@gmx.net

The Artist Haven

I love how God took my hurt and rejection and made beauty. God knows no limit to how He expresses Himself or how He displays His creativity through us. Not many people realise the innate ability we have to be creative, even in our day-to-day ordinary lives. The next story you'll read about is Gushiv, she's a make-up artist who understands what it means to express creativity in unexpected ways. While our canvases may look different, our heart to follow after God through our art remains the same.

Dedication

I dedicate my chapter to my amazing parents and my grandmother. They always taught me to have dignity and the importance of respecting ourselves, not letting anyone put down our values; working hard and smart for whatever we want to do in life. Just like them, working hard toward their life goals. They also set an example for me on how to love my life.

My parents have always supported my dreams since a young age, especially my dad - he was always supporting me and believing in me by giving me all the funds to learn all my artistry skills locally and overseas. My Father had much faith in me and trusted me to let me fly around the world without overly worrying about whether I could succeed or not. My parents kept a copy of my magazine article at home, to show all their relatives and friends how they felt proud of my achievements.

I am so blessed and grateful for their love and support.
— Gushiv D'Arcy

The Devil Can't Buy Your Soul:
Keeping your Heart Clean

Gushiv D'Arcy Ryan
Founder of Gushiv Organics

Byron Bay, Hinterland, Australia, NSW

"I believe in God as I believe the sun had risen,
Not because I can see it, but because by way of it.
I can see everything else."
~ C.S. Lewis[26]

The Hook

We have been given everything we need from Mother Earth; She is filled with riches and treasures that we are so blessed to have available.

We can take these gifts for granted and become selfish in our use of them. There comes a moment in life when we are all tempted to use or keep these resources for our own needs. This is where we are given the freedom to choose how we use these gifts. I have been faced with a similar situation when I could have chosen to take business opportunities that boosted my career in exchange for giving them pleasure, which went against all my values as an individual. In these situations where power and wealth were the temptations that were on offer and I chose

---

[26] Goodreads.com. (2023). Lewis, C.S. Quotable Quotes. Retrieved from: https://www.goodreads.com/quotes/660-i-believe-in-christianity-as-i-believe-that-the-sun

to lean on my faith instead and the gift of my inner strength to get me through. You are not alone in these temptations that we face in life.

I have worked on the international circuit in makeup and design for many years and I have been given opportunities to gain more wealth and influence in exchange for things that would undermine my dignity and worth as a woman. On the outside, the offers look enticing, but there always seems to be a catch at the expense of my own morals and values. Working for worldwide famous figures sometimes you can find yourself at their beck and call to the point where they can walk all over you and when things don't go well you get the blame for not completing the work.

There was a situation where I worked on set with a famous singer and as the make-up crew were running around after him, I decided to confront him and have him sit down so we could complete the work on time. Sometimes you must stand up for yourself in an industry that does not seem to mind walking all over people to get the job done.

Despite coming face to face with temptation on numerous occasions, I have had a strength and force behind me, my faith in God and the values ingrained into me by my heritage. It's thanks to these foundations that I have turned away from the temptation and chose to value and honor the riches of the earth over everything else.

My Transition
Not many people have the courage to pursue what they love, let alone be intentional with how they use the gifts that they have

been given. Imagine a world where we all lived according to the gifts we have been given. Eyes would be brighter, smiles would be wider, and the world would flourish like that of a river; where life within it would be swarming with fish, the lilies would be flowering, the trees growing and animals able to drink from a fresh stream. There would be a balance within the world where every aspect, like the river would complement the other and so, too, would all the gifts, if realized and utilized, when used as one.

This is the desire that our world has for us; that we live to our fullest potential, giving back what we have been given. I have ventured on this path for many years. I embraced the freedom of this choice, to do what I love. I would not say it is an easy path to take, but the result is utter freedom and overflowing joy.

From a young age, it wasn't only my cultural background that inspired me to pursue my dreams. It was also the encounters and industry types I stepped into. Realizing that the world is a dangerous place at times, I was filled with more unnecessary temptations than I thought I would be. However, I came to understand that if I lean not on my own understanding and trust in a greater plan, I can pursue my passions and live my life to the fullest.

My Journey

From as early as I can remember, I have always loved to enhance something by transforming it and making it beautiful. Makeup helped me to do this. I cannot count the number of times I would subject my poor family members allowing me to practice and build upon specific skills such as: learning how to apply eye shadow and defining line tones, making sure basic skin care was done and applied before beginning the design, and ensuring contouring and foundation are just right. They may have disagreed at first, but eventually, everyone wanted a makeover.

I discovered my passion for the beauty and hair industry and despite the voices trying to discourage my pursuit of this dream. I did not give up. I graduated from a local beauty school as a make-up artist and hair stylist in Taiwan and I held my can-do attitude from the very beginning.

It pays to listen to your heart and believe in the incredible gifts that you have worked very hard to cultivate. If I had ignored them, I would not have had the incredible opportunities and doors that opened for me.

Where has this passion taken me? It's taken me to places where dreams are made by working alongside incredible influencers, artists, and brands all around the world. I have had the privilege of working with international productions, advertising, and fashion shows. Freelance show are my go-to as a makeup artist, coinciding with brands like Giorgio Armani, YSL,Shu Uemura, Lancome, Guerlain, MAC, Christian Dior and so on.

As a woman, it has always been a challenge within these industries, but I have an ambitious heart; a gift I am grateful to God for. The hardest challenge is often what other people think of you and your work. When you focus on what others think, it is easy to become discouraged and hopeless, which can get you down. Sometimes I struggled looking at the brilliantly talented artists around me and found myself comparing my work to theirs or finding that I was not moving forward and not as many doors to career opportunities were coming my way I would question if my work and approach were good enough for the industry.

I wondered if I would ever be recognized as an artist for my work? When business opportunities seemed to be too ambitious or particular people wanted something in exchange for more fame and recognition, I would doubt my ability to make something of myself in such a competitive industry. I had to remind myself this is where God is my closest friend and He will never leave my side. He encouraged me when I was down and warned me when the choices I could have made were not good for me. With His help, I worked through the doubts that surrounded me, and as a result, I excelled. I have been sponsored by Yves Saint Laurent, Guerlain, and Jean Paul Gaultier as well as working for all the veejays for Channel V.

The more exposure I received while being in the midst of fashion, beauty, and the like, the more the pleasures began to knock on the door, asking if I would be interested in them. Some of the individuals in this industry would question my loyalty. Being a woman, you do stick out and there seems to be this tendency to take advantage of our sex. Wherever money and power are offered there seems to be this tendency for male leadership to be exploited and stereotyped. Women seem to be categorized, especially in the world of fame, as only meant to be in the home and looking after the family. The leadership and matters of business seem to only remain within the power of men.

When a woman, like me, begins to work in this industry and make a name for herself, men are often preferred to women as this is not their place to be, even if society has begun to accept that women can work and lead as well. So, I stuck out as a businesswoman and artist and had to work harder to resist being used and easily taken advantage of by the stereotyped "men," who exploited their leadership positions. As a result of these stereotypes, some producers or businessmen asked me if I was there for a good time, whilst others offered sexual pleasures for more exclusive opportunities.

Each of us can encounter a moment to indulge in these pleasures and leave us exposed to be tempted. I came face to face every day with such decisions, offering me anything and everything for free. But it truly doesn't make you free. Thanks to my faith, morals and values, and understanding of where these indulgences could lead me. I am quick reassure anyone who asks that I am here to work.

I was approached one day and asked to go to lunch with the producers who had seen my work with Kelly Rowland at the time. One of the top five richest men in China joined us and together the gentlemen wanted to sponsor me to go to Bangkok for two weeks as a makeup artist for a very important film. These are doors that opened to me through my hard work and meeting a variety of people. I accepted and worked as a make-up artist on the film "Into the Sun," starring some huge Hollywood names. I was working with the lead actress who is a well-known Taiwanese model based in Japan, and this two-week gig in Bangkok expected me to do more make-up coordinating and act as a personal assistant for several people.

One of the blockbuster Hollywood names himself was impressed with my five languages and technical expertise and asked me to be his personal assistant. This is where having a solid foundation in faith is necessary to overcome what people can throw at you. The catch was that I might be expected to sleep with him for him to follow through on his offer.

As a young woman, I remained professional, smiled, and laughed it off. The film director also asked me to come to Hollywood to assist with another film as well as asked me out. There seemed to be a hidden agenda, but I remained firm in my boundaries, and he respected my decision. It is not always an easy process, because at the same time your career hangs in the balance. Playing the game is what the industry tried to get me to do, but I realized I didn't need to sell my soul to be professional and successful. Instead, holding onto my integrity was the key.

Challenges like these can weigh you down and plague you with doubt about pursuing your dream. But when you put your mind to something and keep persevering, you can achieve your goals and dreams and accomplish what your heart desires. When a friend asked me to speak on their behalf for London Fashion Week because they were only accepting men, I decided to convince the staff to hire me. Bold and courageous is not easy, but I faced the uncertainty and I stepped out of my comfort zone. As a result, I was able to grab the opportunity with sheer determination. My confidence in my gifts to do what I do best and go for opportunities where I can grow has all happened because I believed in myself.

My gifts and talents have taken me on a journey around the world. I have worked for some incredible and recognizable global brands, worked alongside some worldwide famous people including Michael Bublé, and Kelly Rowland. I met the love of my life and moved to numerous places in pursuit of this career and my husband's work. If it were not for my faith, my cultural background, and my personal areas of growth, I would not be where I am today.

Today, I have learned the skill of marketing and advertising techniques from around the world and set up my Organic Skin Care designed and formulated by myself and Echo Tourism Business from my home in Byron Bay, Hinterland countryside. Settling down and having our son, I realised that after receiving so much, I wanted to give back much more. Embracing everything natural that Mother Earth has gifted me has been my sole focus from the beginning. Opening our large property to glamping opportunities for tourists and guests is a great way for me to love and cherish my family whilst continuing to grow and help others.

If there is anything I have learned throughout my life and career it is that you are not meant to settle down and stop learning. I will never stop learning and the key to this is to remain humble. You never know when something unexpected can happen, so it is important to be prepared. When a friend of mine suddenly went blind, it shattered his ability to enjoy life. He used to be such a healthy and well-spoken salesman and this unexpected challenge crumpled his ability to get back up again because he did not have the hope that faith brings and restores to us when at our worst. One of the hardest challenges, when you are facing obstacles, is accepting the pain that comes with it. How we think and approach each bump in the road will determine the type of experience we have. Thus, my friend's mentality had nothing positive to drag him out of this place of helplessness, he had moral support, but not the kind of capacity to restore his soul. It was a blessing when I met my friend and was able to share my love for God and inspire hope in his life again.

I can relate to his experience completely. Have you ever heard the saying that "God will never give you more than you can handle?" I've experienced numerous seasons of joy and tribulation, and this phrase has really helped shape the person I am today. At the ripe age of twenty-six one of my eyes had a cornea ulcer which left me in the hospital for two to three months. Hospitals in general are challenging places to be, let alone to have to stay there for a couple of days or even a few months. I was dependent on the care of the nurses and doctors to stop the infection from spreading. Every day I received an injection in my eye along with morphine to fight the extremely overwhelming pain.

Not only was this a huge obstacle for me, but in 2021, during the COVID-19 pandemic lockdowns, my husband underwent a very serious and life-endangering surgery to remove a brain tumour and both of us lost our fathers. As a new mom and young wife, the reality of my husband's condition and the uncertainty it brought to my heart presented a unique challenge, in itself. The challenge was to persevere even when things appeared to be out of my control. There were sleepless nights, and I can recall the many times I would just cry with the overwhelming sensation of the weight I carried.

The difference for me, which helped me persevere and maintain a determined attitude was my faith. When you feel out of control you can easily lose hope and even struggle to see a way forward which can feel lonely, but my relationship with God gave me this underlying peace that I would be okay. Doctors kept repeating that I might go blind from this infection, and I was always thinking that I could lose my husband at any moment and our son be left without a father Even though I experienced this uncertainty and felt anxious at times, I did not let it overwhelm me as I remained firm, holding on to the belief that God had my back, my belief, made the burden a little easier.

From these challenges that have arisen in my life, my faith has been like the safety net that prevents me from falling. The notion that I am not alone is all the strength I need to have to stay encouraged. Yet, even in the aftermath of this healing, my mental health was challenged, which led me down paths of depression where I sometimes felt helpless. I remember the core verse from scripture that I held onto like a single golden thread, my lifeline, Psalm 23:4: "Even though I walk through the valley of the shadow of death, I will fear no evil, for you are with me; your rod and your staff, they comfort me." My God has always been my best friend and the only thing that made sense at that time was him and my faith. Because of this relationship and personal faith, I came through six to eight months of recovery and gained some of my autonomy back as well as seeing my husband survive surgery and our families move through the pain of a great loss.

These experiences have taught me humility, trust, and ultimately to cling to my faith just like a child would to their parents. It was here that I learned how to see the positive side of suffering and it transformed my experience of the world.

My perception of life always remains new and exciting because of the new lessons I'm constantly being taught. I still have so many dreams I wish to pursue. Writing a book, enhancing my skincare business, growing a large fruit and vegetable garden for people in need on my property, and building a place of retreat for individuals to come and rejuvenate are just a few of these dreams.

What is the key for a secure and strong foundation to build our lives upon? I recommend spending time with God in prayer. It is a priceless conversation that requires just a couple of words to start such as, "Hi Heavenly Daddy, this is…" Like a friend, tell him anything and everything on your heart and you will be surprised at how your life can be transformed. You will have someone whom you can rely upon 24/7 and 7 days a week. You can tell him anything, and He is the only person in the world who will not judge you nor fight with you. He will listen and be that comfort you seek that no one else in this world can give. He will be honest with you and challenge you to grow, but He won't push you, He will only encourage you and let you know of all the good that comes from making those tough decisions. Ultimately, He leaves the choice up to you. He will always come through on His promises and will make you see the world in a new light. He will share your burdens and relieve the stress and anxiety when you feel overwhelmed and tired. In this way you have room to breathe, space to grow and the eyes to see the world with love.

The possibilities are endless when one continues to pray and dream. To make the most of what we have here on earth, to truly be free, don't be afraid of change, be open to learning, and set those goals so you can strive for more goals and dreams to come. In this way, your life will be bright and fulfilling.

Founder, Gushiv Organics
Gushiv D'Arcy Ryan

"A Heavenly Match"

Using what we have here on Earth,
we can create something amazing.
We have all we will ever need from Mother Earth –
our shared heritage.
We are Royalty from ancient times who have
been blessed with all the Earth's riches;
Our treasures are here on Earth; A Heaven here for us all.
~ Gushiv D'Arcy Ryan

About The Author

Gushiv D'Arcy Ryan is the Founder and Creator of Gushiv Organics. She is your creative, professional, or personal aspirations and how you support others.

Gushiv believes that skincare is not just about the "here and now" but the long term health of skin. Preserving the health of your skin with ingredients that have naturally been around forever. Our planet has all we need for life to thrive.

Her skincare products use native, organic ingredients sourced from Mother Nature. She and her team use the latest environmentally friendly modern scientific extraction methods to preserve the phyto-nutritional benefits of Mother Nature's botanical ingredients and transfer them to your skin.

Gushiv uses some of the best Australian Native ingredients renowned for their benefits for skin care. We are pleased to introduce you to our Australian Timeless Collection from the ancient land of Gondwana.

Gushiv lives with her husband of 13 years and their son who is a toddler. He loves life and is growing up in his mother's footsteps with the love of the land and learning the beauty of life and the environment around us.

FIND ME:

Website: Australian Native Organic Skincare | Gushiv Organics
Facebook: Gushiv Skincare-
https://www.facebook.com/gushivorgan
Instagram: *@gushivorganic*
Email: *Contact@gushiv.com*
Book in for a Chat: https://calendly.com/gushiv-skin-
consultation/20min/?month=2023-04

The Artist Haven

Following God is an adventure, that's for sure. You never quite know where God is going to lead you when you say yes to Him! My co-author, Tim, knows this all too well. He shares candidly about his experiences following God in the various seasons of life.

Dedication

To Martha, my beloved wife, and my wonderful life mate, with whom I have journeyed through many of life's adventures as we followed after Jesus Christ, our Lord!
~Tim

Walking Behind Jesus:
The Art of Listening and Trusting God

Tim Bhajjan
Watercolor Artist & Christian Life Coach

Arizona, USA

Introduction

In this chapter I would like to take you on a journey with me. Along the way, we will discover some markers that led to the unearthing of a reservoir of great wealth. I am a professional watercolour artist who creates paintings and teaches workshops. I am also a Christian Life Coach who gives online coaching sessions. My wife and I run a nonprofit organization called Split Rock.

Undergirding all that I do are lessons I learned while undergoing a unique set of experiences the Lord brought into my life. As I went through what I now see as three developmental stages, my relationship deepened with God. First, I began to recognize God's voice. Second, I not only heard His instructions; but also started to obey Him. And finally, there developed an art form of listening and trusting Him as I moved forward. It is my prayer that as you read about my experiences, you will gain insights and inspiration for your own deepened walk with Jesus!

Hearing Him

I was an international student from India who was about to complete my final year at Bethel Seminary in St. Paul, Minnesota. Along with the weight of studies and graduation that year, I also wanted to meet my life mate that year and had prayed fervently about this matter.

One Sunday morning in September 1990, I had the opportunity to attend a church service during which an announcement was made that a short-term mission team was being formed to go to Haiti. My ears perked up because I was studying world missions but had never ventured on a mission trip. But there was a risk that I would have to face. After completing my Master's program, I would stay in the U.S. to begin a doctoral program at Trinity Seminary in Deerfield, Illinois. As I pondered going on this mission trip, I knew that leaving the country on my student visa could jeopardize further studies, as I could be denied reentry into the U.S. Human wisdom would dictate for me not to take the risk. On the way home from the service I sensed God directing me to go. This became a matter of prayer for me and I wrestled back and forth with God. It finally came down to putting my trust in God and choosing what He wanted me to do. I concluded that if I were to be denied reentry, then I would either go back to India and carry on whatever work God was going to show me, or He would make a way for me to return to the US and continue my studies. So, in faith, I went to Haiti on a short-term mission trip.

It was New Year's Eve and I found myself alone with God, disappointed that He had not answered my prayer. In the background, I could hear my teammates gathering together to pray in the new year during the final moments of 1990. We bowed our heads in prayer and I heard the distinct, small voice of God say to me: "Tim, open your eyes and look right across from you. The woman you see straight across from you is going to be your mate." I quickly opened my eyes and saw the leader of the group, Martha. I shut my eyes and gratefully thanked God for answering my prayer.

Shortly after arriving back, I got together with Martha under the guise of talking about the logistics for the Haiti mission trip, but this was in fact our first date, and from then on we steadily dated for the next three months before becoming engaged. It was during this time that Martha shared with me that God was also doing a work in her heart to prepare her for our marriage. Six months later we were married!

During our wedding ceremony, two roses dropped from Martha's bouquet. Martha and I noted their significance – to us these symbolized the dedication of our lives as living sacrifices to God. From here on, we believed that together we were crossing the threshold of an incredible adventurous journey with Jesus Christ.

Listening and Obeying Him

I grew up in a Christian home in India. My father was a pastor in the Methodist Church, as were his father and grandfather. I wanted to follow in their footsteps and a miraculous opening came for me to pursue theological studies at Bethel Seminary, in Minnesota, USA. From there I began a Ph.D. Program in Intercultural studies. Within two years, I had completed all my coursework; and was getting ready to settle on a topic for my dissertation.

In all matters, big or small, I have tried to consult with the Lord for His will. As I prayed for guidance, the heavens seemed to be shut tight. I continued to call out to God and, many days later, I heard Him ask me a question, "Are you happy here?" The question started to haunt me. Day and night, whether at school studying in the library or at home, with my wife and daughter, the question kept burning in my heart and mind: "Was I happy here?"

One afternoon I set all aside and pondered my response. I weighed all matters, previous life experiences, life in the US and here in Illinois and slowly a pattern started emerging and with it a deep sense of conviction. For the first time, I started realizing what I had done. It had been a subtle shift in focus that had led to a different trajectory than where I actually wanted to be and with it came the deeper realization, an answer to His question. "No, I wasn't happy here. I was no longer a ministering person, caring for others, sharing about Jesus Christ with them, Instead, I had become a nocturnal creature. Night and day, like the other students, spending long hours burrowed in the library, researching facts and figures, collecting quotes to sound profound and conversing with professors deemed to be sages in classrooms, but devoid of any contact with the real world.

I bowed my head, stunned by this realization when I heard God again. He explained how this pursuit of profundity had steered me off course toward idolatry. In 1977, under conviction for my sins, I had given my heart to the Lord, with such fervor and sincerity, and had experienced the flooding joy of the presence of His Spirit. Now I understood that I had abandoned Him and His plans for my life and had started pursuing my own.

He clearly laid it on the ground, no compromise... if I wanted Him back, then I needed to terminate my Ph.D. program and follow Him into what He had for me. Tears stung my eyes; my mouth was dry and my heart ached deeply. I knew that this was what it would cost me to follow Him. It was a hard thing God was asking and it was not easy to let go, but I did.

My wife and I were in ongoing prayer asking God for direction about what to do next. One day, in my spirit, God spoke, "Lancashire." We did not know where this was; but came to find it to be in the NW part of England. We found a map in the library and came back home to seek God about where He wanted us to go in Lancashire, a place where we knew no one. I got "Lancaster" and my wife got nearby Morecambe Bay. Both of these places turned out to be significant places in and through our lives.

At this point, we had a one and a half year old daughter, Mary, and Martha was again pregnant. We had virtually no funds and were instructed by the Lord not to ask anyone for funds. He gave us His promise that He would continuously provide everything we needed as we sought first His Kingdom and followed Him, in faith.

One day a woman called and asked how much we needed for our airfares. We still needed the full amount and when she was told the figure, she responded, "I'm putting a check in the mail tomorrow."

This is an example of how God provided miraculously throughout the whole process of getting ready and during our time in Lancashire. Other provisions included: a contact person in Lancashire; a three-month visa for the UK on my Indian passport; continual, unusual leading and favor; ongoing food supplies and funds; and a lovely home in a beautiful cottage. The property was set in the tiny village of Borwick, on farmland that included a canal and walking paths. People would come from all over for encouragement and prayer.

Four months later our son, Paul, was born. Everything about the experience was idyllic, so we were surprised when Martha and I began to sense a stirring that God was going to send us someplace else. We began to seek the Lord for His leading. One Sunday evening, I went to hear a message being given at a church service in Morecambe. During this time, God began to speak to me about Israel and I sensed He would be sending us there. When I got ready to leave the building to head back home, I heard my name being called. I turned around and saw one of the ladies from the congregation approaching me and carrying the huge bouquet of flowers that had been placed at the altar. She graciously handed them to me and said, "Tim, please take these home to Martha from us all!"

When I returned to the cottage, I came right into the living room to see Martha and to let her know what the Lord had spoken to me. Martha was not happy with this news and let me know that the Lord had not told her that. Now the bottom line for both Martha and me is to be in the center of God's will. So after handing Martha the bouquet, which she placed on the floor beside her chair, we spent some time in prayer about Israel. What I didn't know at the time was Martha's silent interaction with God, "Lord, if this is really your plan for us, then please have two flowers fall from the bouquet so I can know without a doubt that it is You who is taking us into this dangerous part of the world."

The next thing I heard was Martha saying over and again, "I knew they were going to be there! I knew they were going to be there!" She was pointing at the two flowers that had fallen from the bouquet onto the carpet during our prayer time. Martha was now certain that God had revealed to us the next step we were to take.

We had similar circumstances as when we were given the instructions to go to the UK. We had no financial provision to travel to Israel; no relationships, no place to live; and additionally, we could not speak the language! But God came through again, every time and in every need with: finances, without our asking people; places to live, favor, new relationships; and ultimately a home in the center of Jerusalem where people could come for encouragement and prayer. We lived in Israel for 5½ years before being led back to England for another 2½ years. God brought us back to the U.S. in 2003 and for the next fourteen years, I served as a pastor in three churches in Minnesota. Then the Lord called me out of pastoring to become a Life Coach and a professional watercolour artist.

Developing the Art of Listening and Trusting Him
It was the fall of 2017 and as we sought the Lord for the next step He showed me the picture of tall, paper mâché palm trees and then the letters "AZ." Martha and I sensed God was sending us to Tucson, Arizona. Also at this time, the Lord directed us to get training to become Christian life coaches and to start a nonprofit organization, called Split Rock.

God made a way for us to travel in a caravan of three cars in the company of friends who go to Arizona each winter. When we first arrived in Arizona we were provided places to stay in friends' homes. During this season of transition, I continued to pursue my interest in watercolour painting, and Martha and I worked to establish Split Rock. It became important for me to find a place to live in close proximity to the Southern Arizona Watercolour Guilds (SAWG) Gallery. SAWG consists of over 300 watercolour and mixed media artists and it is a nonprofit organization that helps artists like me to grow and improve their abilities as artists.

One day Martha asked me, "Tim, if everything was provided for you, what would you most desire to do in the days ahead?" I gave her question some thought for a few moments and then replied, "I would love to become a professional watercolour artist." Martha was supportive and yet quite surprised by my answer, as she had assumed my answer would be connected with our new Split Rock Life Coaching work.

I had been drawn to doing watercolours while we were living in Jerusalem and when we moved to Morecambe UK, I had an opportunity to be part of a watercolour painting group that met in Heysham, a nearby town. Later during my fourteen years in ministry working as a full-time pastor I would paint on my day off.

Doing watercolours as a hobby was a welcome rest after a week of activity from my work as a pastor of a church. At church a majority of my time was spent interacting with other people, staff meetings, counseling sessions, visitations, spending time in study for my Sunday sermons and preparation for teaching classes that I was going to do that month. In contrast to this my painting time allowed me to focus on a creative activity that I enjoyed immensely, it was taking place in the quietness of my home where interaction with others was minimal and it was restorative, renewing me sufficiently to begin my next week's responsibilities on a fresh note.

When the Lord opened the door for me to make my hobby into a full-time activity the "one-day" allocation expanded from three to five days of immersion in this creative field. I started spending more time improving my skills, diligently setting time aside each day to practice drawing and painting. I also began learning more about watercolours through reading books, watching videos, taking workshops from other artists and so on. Later I created and launched my website and began engaging with potential clients on a variety of social media platforms. I also began selling my artwork and got acquainted with the fundamentals of marketing.

In 2023 I began to teach watercolour classes, hold workshops locally in Tucson and become a co-author in writing and sharing my story through this book – Artists' Haven. Becoming a professional allowed me to invest quality time in these aspects of my development as an artist.

The point shows and workshops that SAWG offered helped me immensely to improve. Soon I became a Juried Member. Then in 2021, I became a Signature Member and in 2023, the Guild recognized me as a Saguaro Fellow. I started selling my watercolours in Yuma, AZ and at SAWG's Gallery. In 2022, I taught a beginner watercolour class at SAWG and this year at an RV Resort in Tucson. I also developed a series of eight two-day workshops called "The Next Step Watercolour Workshop." These workshops help artists to learn, grow and develop their skills and move them toward creating a juried watercolour painting. I intentionally work with small groups of up to eight people, so that I can spend quality time with each artist. The combination of the emphasis on experiential learning and my coaching skills benefits each artist, regardless of where they are on their artistic journey.

On this journey of becoming an artist and a life coach, I discovered a reservoir of great wealth. The art of listening to Jesus and trusting Him to lead the way is best developed by walking one step behind Him and being attentive to what He says. I get to apply the art of listening and trusting Jesus during times of coaching and interaction with artists. Here are the words of Jesus that sum up what I had discovered.

> *Walk with Me and work with Me—watch how I do it.*
> *Learn the unforced rhythms of grace.*
> *I won't lay anything heavy or ill-fitting on you.*
> *Keep company with Me and*
> *you'll learn to live freely and lightly*
> *(Matt.10:28-30 The Message)*

Over the past six years, I have experienced how to "live freely and lightly" as I keep company with Jesus. He has filled my heart with a deep sense of satisfaction and purpose, and I get to use the gifts He has placed in me.

In closing, let me challenge you to press into God to hear what He is saying to you. God loves to communicate with His people. What new thing is He inviting you to do with Him? May you choose to listen, obey, and begin to develop a unique artform that impacts others around you for God's glory.

Tim Bhajjan

"Lifted Up" - My rendition of the "Christ the Redeemer" statue in Rio de Janeiro, Brazil.

"Turning the Page"
A deeply engrossed reader bound to an engaging chapter!

"Pensive Reflections of Life"

About The Author

Tim Bhajjan is a watercolour artist who has lived in Arizona since 2018. He is a Signature member and a Saguaro Fellow at the Southern Arizona Watercolour Guild, Tucson, AZ. He is also a member of the American Watercolour Society and the National Watercolour Society.

Tim has been painting with watercolours for over fifteen years and professionally for the last five years. His first art exhibition, *Desert of Hope,* was held at Yuma Art Center in March 2019. Since then, Tim has participated in several shows and exhibitions held at the Southern Arizona Watercolour Guild's Gallery in Tucson. Tim's paintings have also been displayed at Arizona State University's Watts College of Public Service and Community Solutions in Phoenix, AZ and at the Intersection Gallery in Gilbert, AZ.

Tim has attended workshops with prominent artists such as Mary Whyte, Tony Couch and Graham Berry. He has developed a style of fusion in his paintings, which incorporates elements of realism and abstraction. Tim has also created biographical art, which shares key aspects of a person's life through visually creative watercolour paintings.

Tim holds Next Step Watercolour Workshops to encourage beginner and Intermediate level artists to develop their skills and touch new heights in their artwork. He also teaches an Introduction to Watercolour class at Voyager RV Resort in Tucson during the months of January-March.

In Fall of 2022 Tim's painting, *Red Hot,* was selected to be on the book cover of *Those Who Are Gone,* by Lawrence F. Lihosit. His watercolour, *Fargo* won the Best of Show award at the Last Impressions Show held recently at Southern Arizona

Watercolor Guild's Gallery in Tucson. And his painting *Juicer,* was accepted by Juror Jackson Boelts, Professor Emeritus in Art at the University of Arizona, Tucson, to be part of the 2023 Arizona Aqueous XXXVII show at Tubac Center of the Arts, in Arizona.

Find Me:
Facebook: https://www.facebook.com/tim.bhajjan
Instagram: https://www.instagram.com/timbhajjan/
Website: www.timbhajjanart.com

The Artist Haven

While I paint I with watercolour, DeAnne paints with her words. She is a singer, songwriter and her zeal to honour the Lord with her creative gifts is inspiring. Her story is one that shows how her spiritual roots give her confidence to seek God's creative plans.

Dedication

I dedicate my chapter to my sweet, beautiful mother, Mary Rose Eastwood Morrell and my late brilliant father, Raymond David Morrell. My parents taught me about Jesus when I was young and steered me towards a life of truth and perfect love. They were always there for me, encouraging me to follow my dreams and my heart. Thank you for always believing in me and for your endless supply of uplifting words. I know what it is to be loved without condition. Your unconditional love has always made me feel safe and at home. Thank you Mom and Dad, I love you.

I also dedicate this chapter to my amazing, handsome, intelligent, and talented son, Joe; I am so proud of you! And to my grandsons, Jude and Rowan. You are all shining stars and I love you.

A special thanks to Armando Giacometti for all that you've done for me. Blessings...

M. DeAnne Morrell

Cultivate the Beauty Within

M. DeAnne Morrell
Founder/Owner/Coach,
Nocturnal Red Music

Canada

"It is not the critic who counts; not the man who points out how the strong man stumbles, or where the doer of deeds could have done them better. The credit belongs to the man who is actually in the arena, whose face is marred by dust and sweat and blood; who strives valiantly; who errs, who comes short again and again, because there is no effort without error and shortcoming; but who does actually strive to do the deeds; who knows great enthusiasms, the great devotions; who spends himself in a worthy cause; who at the best knows, in the end, the triumph of high achievement, and who at the worst, if he fails, at least fails while daring greatly, so that his place shall never be with those cold and timid souls who neither know victory nor defeat."
~ *Theodore Roosevelt*[27]

Treetop Memoirs

"Redheaded cooty girl! Redheaded cooty girl!" I heard as I took my spot in Four Square for fourth-grade recess. *Oh no... it's my nemesis again*, I thought, *and she's come to mock my red hair and freckles.*

---

[27] Roosevelt, T. (23Apr1910). Excerpt from speech, "Citizenship In A Republic" Sorbonne, Paris, France, April 23, 1910

"You look like you have cooties all over your skin" she'd say, "and you're as pale as Casper."

"Well at least Casper was friendly!" I'd cry. (Casper the Friendly Ghost is a famous animated cartoon series that was popular when I was a child.)

"Casper has cooties! Casper has cooties!" she'd chant. (Kids can be so cruel).

She's pushing me and knows it. It's starting to happen... I can feel myself getting very angry and then, BAMM! I slammed the ball at Todd in square 3 and he's out and I move up!

Like many, my hurt often turned to anger, but for me, it has almost always been productive anger. A "success is the best revenge" mindset if you will. As a child, my naturally red hair, freckles, and pale skin were a constant source of mockery for me and made me feel very alone and unwanted. I would frequently run away and climb trees. Nature's tranquility was where I would find peace and I would consistently write poems and sing to myself. It was then that I first discovered my artist's haven, and how I would go there in my mind over the years to pull out the talent God put in me.

Miss American Coed

"Morrell, on in 10!" the stagehand yelled into the greenroom where almost 100 Miss American Coed pageant hopefuls were gathered, of which I was one. I had just turned 18, and my son, Joseph David, was only 1 year old. Single and a mother, I had entered the Miss American Coed Pennsylvania State pageant. I had entered the talent competition as well, and I was singing and playing piano. I had put a melody to my brother Martin's words:

> "I take a walk and then I sit down.
> At last, it's true I have been found.
> God with His beautiful, magnificent grace
> Has cleverly found my hiding place. "

The lights dimmed and I walked out on stage and sat down at the grand piano in front of thousands of onlookers and began to play and sing our original song. There was complete silence as I performed. *Wow!* I thought. *What an amazing feeling to be listened to.* When I sang the final note, the audience erupted with thunderous, loud clapping and I could have sworn I heard my brothers, Marty and Kevin, howling over the crowd. I was beaming. *This is it*, I realized. This is my true calling. *I now know that my life must include singing and performing*, I surmised.

The head judge proclaims, "And the winner of the overall talent portion for Miss American Coed Pennsylvania State is..."

Could it be me? I asked myself.

"DeAnne Morrell for her singing and original composition."

Wow! It is me! I was so excited that I had won the talent portion and also received a big ole trophy and 200 bucks.

Then the head judge proclaims, "And the winner of Miss American Coed Pennsylvania State is..."

Not me. That's when I knew that it wasn't about the beauty outside of me that God wanted, but that it was about the beauty within that I needed to cultivate, harness, and ride.

New Life Island, The Grateful Dead, and The Grammys

I was raised in a secure and loving Biblical home with strong Christian parents who protected and provided for me. As the youngest and only girl of 3 children, my parents doted on me

149

and safeguarded me. I accepted Christ as my Saviour when I was around 8. My two older brothers and I got along well and were the best of friends growing up. We all went to a private Christian school and would go to New Life Island Christian camp In New Jersey in the summers. I remember singing:

"I am a promise. I am a possibility.
I am a promise with a capital P
I am a great big bundle of potentiality
And I am learning to hear God's voice
And I am trying to make the right choices
I'm a promise to be anything He wants me to be."

I looked up to my older brothers so when my oldest brother rebelled against the church at 16 and began smoking pot and following the Grateful Dead around, I too, followed suit. We were like two peas in a pod. We had moved to Pennsylvania because in those days my mother and a doctor of science from the Fox Chase Cancer Center had started their own laboratory raising germ-free, albino rats and mice for cancer research in Amish country and she needed to be closer to her work. They had 10 rooms filled with hundreds of rats and mice that needed to be fed and changed constantly. My brothers and I all worked at the lab we soon coined "The Rat Farm."

I was the ripe age of 13 when I started working there. I had managed to save up enough money to buy my own airline ticket to California as well as several Grateful Dead tickets from their business headquarters in San Rafael for their summer concerts in Berkeley and Ventura. I flew alone and met up with my brother in Pasadena where we spent the next two weeks hitch-hiking from Santa Barbara to Berkeley and back down to

Ventura following the Grateful Dead. The adventures we had on Pacific Highway One alone could fill another book. After returning from my Californian adventure, my Christian parents were not impressed with my partying lifestyle and I was sent off to rehab.

Soon after, at age 15, I met the man who would father my son. I was just 16 when I got pregnant with Joe. Having been raised in a Christian home that preached against sex until marriage, being pregnant out of wedlock at 16 was hard for my folks. But they loved me and saw me through. At 18, I graduated from cosmetology school, passed boards, and received my license in cosmetology.

I rededicated my life back to Christ and would go on to spend my entire 20s completely sober and touring with my music. Soon after my re-dedication to Christ, at 19, I met the man that would become my first husband. I had entered a local talent show and his band was in it, too. We formed a band and soon after recorded our first demo. A few years after that we recorded our first full-length CD at Digital Dog Studios in Philadelphia, PA. This CD opened doors that led all the way to the Gram **M. DeAnne Morrell** ⟩ and we were being interviewed live on many different radio stations.

The video for our song, "The View" was spinning on MTV and other music cable shows. We were asked to join the Recording Academy where I was an active voting member for over 20 years and could attend the Grammys every year. After performing several times at The Bitter End in NYC, a producer who had worked with names like Sting, Madonna, and Tina Turner was in the audience for one of my performances and he signed me to his production company. He produced our next EP.

Songs from this album went on to win several Billboard Certificate of Achievement awards.

My music dream was well on its way but meanwhile, back at the ranch, my 10-year marriage was ending and sorrow over that was often overwhelming. I blew 11 years of sobriety and began to drink. While performing a concert in the Philadelphia area in 1999 there was a truck driver in the audience that would eventually become my second husband. Our lifestyle consisted of parties and good times. It seemed I had gotten away from the Lord and my life of singing. I'd do a show here and there but put singing on the back burner for my marriage. Eventually, the pull was too strong and once again I was back to performing full-time with a variety band and toured regionally. We played 10 to 15 shows a month, every month and I loved it but once again my marriage took a toll. The music was secular and not a lot of worshiping the Lord was going on. Something was missing... I loved the Lord and this life was not fulfilling me anymore.

After my second marriage ended, I was unsure where my life was leading but I knew I needed to lean back into the Lord. I stopped drinking and backed away from performing live. I started teaching voice in a local studio for a few years. Eventually, I moved back to Canada where my family is from and settled into my life there. My terminally ill father came to live with me and I took care of him for two years until his passing in 2020. Covid hit and while in shutdown I started going to a Christian business academy and learned new business skills to take my training online. I founded Nocturnal Red Music where I submit songs to artists, TV, film, etc. as well as teach vocal lessons online via Zoom. I love my simple, sober, Christian life in

Canada where I live in my artist's haven in a remote cabin in the woods with my 3 cats and happiness.

Looking Back Through the Hourglass

I've heard it said that hindsight is 20/20. Sure, it can be far easier to assess and analyze a situation after it has already occurred, instead of in real-time while it's happening. When I look back through the hourglass of my life and ruminate upon how I moved forward through many of my life's situations, I am able to observe certain key methods of operation throughout the years that have routinely sustained me, carried me, and catapulted me forward into my artistic destiny's calling where I can utilize the talents God gave me for not only the furtherance of His kingdom but also the furtherance of my spiritual peace. I truly believe God gives us our talents to use for His glory but also for our peace in our artistic haven. For me, achieving artistic synergy is when I lock into the peace of my artistic haven while performing my talents for the masses and the advancement of the kingdom through music, worship, and praise. Here are 3 of those key methods that helped me most in my artistic journey:

Key 1: Be Angry and Do Not Sin

Looking back, my fourth-grade experience with my nemesis is where I first observed implementing being angry and using it productively. Instead of lashing out at her, I focused on the task at hand more intensely and got Todd out and moved up to the next square. God was molding me from a young age.

He says in Ephesians 4:26-27 NKJV "Be angry, and do not sin: do not let the sun go down on your wrath, nor give place to the devil." Our Father in Heaven gets angry when His righteous standards are violated. If we are to be imitators of God (Ephesians 5:1 NASB) then we too must get angry at what makes God angry, but we must be careful to not sin as our perfect God would not. When we are mad we should check to see if we are mad at what God hates. If we are angry without cause it may give an opening for the Devil to enter our minds and distract us from our calling. When I am angry, sad, happy, or feeling just about any emotion, I go into my artist's haven, start playing piano and singing, and let the music flow. Your emotions can help you develop variety in your art form. Let your anger be productive anger where you can tap into your creative hidden treasures.

Key 2: Focus on What God Says, Not People

When my nemesis would make fun of me because of my red hair, freckles, and pale skin I felt like people hated me because I looked different or funny. When I was 18, a graduate of beauty school, a contestant in the Pennsylvania State Miss American Coed pageant, and a singer on stage... I found people still made fun of me. I was mocked when I thought I looked funny and I was mocked when I grew into my womanhood. Focus on what God says you are and forget about what people say, then go into your artist haven and create.

You are God's masterpiece.
Ephesians 2:10 (NLT)

You are fearfully and wonderfully made.
Psalm 139:14 (KJV)
For the Lord does not see as man sees.
1 Samuel 16:7 (NKJV)
I have loved you with an everlasting love.
Jeremiah 31:3 (NKJV)
He chose us in Him before the foundation of the world.
Ephesians 1:4 (NKJV)
The very hairs of your head are all numbered.
Luke 12:7 (NKJV)
Every good gift and every perfect gift is from above. James
1:17 (KJV)

Key 3: Tap Into Your Creativity

Our creative spirit is certainly a gift from God. But, like any gift, we must open it up and see what's inside. In Genesis 1:1 (NKJV), created is the fifth word of the first verse of the Bible. "In the beginning, God created the heavens and the earth." Matter and space-time continuum spoken into existence by the true and living God. Further in Genesis 1:27 (NKJV), we read, "So God created man in His own image; in the image of God He created him; male and female He created them." God is creative and He made us like Him. How can we tap into the colours of a sunset or the song of a nightingale?

As I am using my art of music for the glory of God, my first step is to pray and ask the Holy Spirit to move within me and use me. Then I reflect on Psalm 46:10 (NKJV), "Be still and know that I am God." I close my eyes and take deep diaphragmatic breaths and focus on the Spirit of the Lord where

He takes me into a deep relaxed state. Being relaxed and focused on the Lord is key to tapping into the creative talent He gave you.

A Creation Made New

2 Corinthians 5:17 (NKJV) says, "Therefore, if anyone is in Christ, he is a new creation; old things have passed away; behold, all things have become new." Since I stopped worrying about people's opinions and began to focus on God's thoughts and plans for me, my life has been amazing. I wake up grateful for each day. I wake up happy and hopeful for the future. Scripture tells us in Jeremiah 29:11(NKJV), "For I know the thoughts that I think toward you, says the Lord, thoughts of peace and not of evil, to give you a future and a hope." God loves us. Accepting and falling in love with Jesus was life-transforming for me. Tapping into the deep love God has for me allows me to be all I can be in Him, to live for Him, and to use my talents to further the Kingdom. I love to write songs and sing praises to my Lord. It brings me immeasurable joy.

Rejoice, Be Glad, and Remain Teachable

"This is the day the LORD has made; We will rejoice and be glad in it"! Psalm 118:24(NKJV) is my life's motto. That and remain teachable. Rejoice, be glad, take action, and make changes where needed. Listen to what the Lord's Word says about you and continually use it to improve yourself.

Are you following the plans God has for your life?

God knows what He wants for us and has the blueprint for our lives drawn up. Our job is to find out what that is through prayer, actively reading God's Word, and following and obeying the commands He puts on our hearts.

"You may not control all the events that happen to you,
but you can decide not to be reduced by them."
~ Maya Angelou[28]

M. DeAnne Morrell

Founder/Owner/Coach, Nocturnal Red Music
M. DeAnne Morrell

ANGEL IN THE BACKYARD
by: M. DeAnne Morrell

I've got an angel in the backyard watching over me
I've got an angel in the backyard
who sees things I can't see
He forever keeps guard over my life both night and day
And carries me up high over the rough stones in my way

Telling me he is my friend
Though I cannot comprehend

---

[28] Goodreads.com. (2023). Quotable Quote. Retrieved from: https://www.goodreads.com/quotes/228308-you-may-not-control-all-the-events-that-happen-to

How he keeps me free from harm
Away from the Devil's arms
He comforts me in times of strife
Fulfilling God's will for my life
And looks upon my Father's face
Beyond Heaven's pearly gates

I've got an angel in the backyard that ministers to me
I've got an angel in the backyard that hones my clarity
He forever gives me strength and unconditional love
While guiding me to inherit God's full kingdom above

I simply smile winsomely
The way my angel intervenes
Satan robs, kills, and destroys
So my angel God employed
To enforce my covenant rights
That Jesus paid for when He died
Conquering the grave to complete
Ensuring Lucifer's defeat

I've got an angel in the backyard, he's by the old birch tree
I've got an angel in the backyard waiting to deliver me
I send forth ministering angels to protect our families
And pray we find rest in the shadow of the Almighty

About The Author

Mary DeAnne Morrell (who goes by DeAnne or Coach MD) is the founder and owner of Nocturnal Red Music. She is an award-winning, multiple instrumentalist, singer, songwriter, Christian recording artist, #1 International Bestselling Author, voiceover artist, high-performance vocal/life coach and graphic artist. For the past 15 years, Coach MD has helped countless vocalists who have been struggling with their singing, to move beyond their physical and psychological barriers and set their voice and spirit free. She is extremely passionate and purpose-driven and believes strongly in helping singers get the voice and confidence of which they dream. In addition to singing, playing piano and congas... DeAnne loves to camp, geocache, hike, kayak, ride motorcycles, scuba dive and tear up the back forty on a wild ATV adventure.

FIND ME:
Facebook: https://www.facebook.com/fundygrrl
Website: https://www.mdmorrell.com
Email: mdmorrell@nocturnalredmusic.ca or
coach@mdmorrell.com
Schedule a Call: https://calendly.com/coachmdmorrell
    Free Gift for the client: https://www.mdmorrell.com/free-gift

The Artist Haven

Our creative confidence is only possible through our relationship with God. My co-author, Melanie shares how she also became bold creatively to pursue different artistic mediums. Using all her artistic endeavours not for her gain, but for God's glory.

Dedication

*I dedicate my chapter to my wonderful husband, Newman.
You are my biggest support, the love of my life and my best
friend. Thank you for always being by my side, making me
smile and making life so sweet! I love you always!*
~Melanie

He Restores My Soul

Melanie Meihua Peeauake
Artist

Australia

"**1** The LORD *is* my shepherd;
I shall not want.
2 He makes me to lie down in green pastures;
He leads me beside the still waters.
3 He restores my soul;
He leads me in the paths of righteousness
For His name's sake." (Psalm 23:1-3)

Psalm 23 has a significant meaning to me; it has helped me through many trials and given me comfort in knowing that God has got me. He holds everything in my life together.

I didn't have a stable home life and grew up in a violent and explosive household. This led me to fall into a deep depression and a lack of identity and self-worth. I felt that I didn't even have a purpose for living. This went on for a few years and carried on to my adult life. I had faith in God, but I didn't have an intimate relationship with Him. I found my identity in getting validation from people and from how I grew up. I was a trapped and broken person who desperately needed God.

My feelings weren't heard when I was growing up, so I almost tried to push them away and suppress them. So I used my art to escape and express what I felt. This was a good outlet, but I had a lot of pain, anger and hate in my heart that my drawings became lifeless. My drawings largely focused on the pain I was feeling inside, and they eventually took the joy from creating.

The defining moment in my life was finding Jesus. I gave my life to Jesus at my youth ministry's summer camp when I was about 14. I was worshipping and suddenly felt the presence of God for the first time; I began crying out of pure joy. One day, I remember being in my room, trying not to be overwhelmed by things going on at home. I was reading my Bible, trying to find answers to my problems, and I read Psalm 23, and a particular phrase jumped out at me, "He restores my soul." I felt an incredible peace wash over me, and I felt God's presence with me. The presence of God was so strong I just felt completely at peace. I took out my sketchbook and began to draw. I drew a girl who was completely at peace, content and calm.

My art transformed, and instead of it focusing on my trauma, it focused on God. This sparked my passion for creating artwork that portrayed the love of God and the love that He gives us. My art is predominantly expressing my love for the beauty of His creation, such as beautiful landscapes, sunsets and flowers, what His love means to me, His character and faithfulness and making handmade gifts for loved ones.

I currently work at my church and Pastor the Youth Ministry with my husband. In addition to art, I'm also passionate about helping people. I attended the youth ministry at my church and I found a community there who loved and supported me. I had people around me who pointed me to Jesus and showed me there was more to life. This church became my home and my family. My life was saved by Jesus there, and due to my upbringing I wanted to help those find their identity in God and to let them know that their past doesn't define them. Now I get the honour of leading that ministry alongside my husband, helping those with my story and leading them to Jesus.

Once I found Jesus and developed that relationship with Him, I was able to find my strength in Him and lean completely on Him. This began my healing journey; God has brought me out of my past and helped me let go of the past. I had a lot of hate and unforgiveness in my heart that I had to let go of. And although my relationship with my parents isn't perfect, I love and honour them.

I used to dislike my own culture because the home I grew up in was the only representation of that. What I had grown up seeing gave me the wrong perspective of my culture. But as I've been on this journey with Jesus, I've grown to love myself and who He has created me to be. God healed this part of my life and even put people around me that empower me and love my culture as well! I have embraced this as part of who I am and now love this about myself, which is where the inspiration for my artist's name came from. Mei Hua is my Chinese name and English middle name. I wanted to take hold of who I am and my culture and incorporate it into something I am passionate about. The word 'Mei' means 'beautiful' in Chinese, and I wanted my artwork to represent the beauty of things that bring me joy. My artist's name represents the beauty of my culture and is part of who I am.

When I began my journey of sharing my art my first step was to just take that leap of faith; I felt like God had put a passion for creativity in my life, and I have always dreamed of sharing it with the world around me. I felt God was putting a strong desire in my heart to share my art with others. What helped me through this journey was my husband and sister supporting me in my art and passions; always cheering me on with every piece I made and with the content I posted.

I decided to start filming my process anytime I started painting, drawing and making artwork. I then started thinking of my artist's name, which became 'by mei'. Ever since I have been uploading my artwork, filming the behind-the-scenes and starting my own Etsy shop.

Here are three keys I think could benefit you in your journey of sharing your creativity.

1. There is only one YOU!
    God designed you and me so intentionally, with every single detail of our lives in mind. He gave us our specific gifts, passions, abilities and ideas for a reason! Recognising this is one of the most important keys to growth because when you know that you were intentionally made to share your creativity with the world and no one else can share what you can, you will be unashamed of your work!
    One thing that was hindering me from starting out was the comparison. I compared myself to other artists who were way ahead of me in their journeys, and it was really discouraging for me to wonder if I even had a chance. I kept praying about this and seeking support from those around me, and eventually, I decided to let the comparison go. This allowed me to recognise that God has given me this passion and desire for creativity and that what I have to share is unique to me! This can still be hard at times, but the key to growing is being confident in

what you have to offer and that God has given you these gifts for a reason!

2. Have a good support system
   Having a support system around me has helped me keep moving forward and staying consistent in my journey as an artist. It can get difficult at times, especially when the artwork you're sharing is not being appreciated or getting much engagement, so you need people around you who will help you to keep going and stay encouraged because there are times when this journey is amazing, and you should have people to celebrate with you!

3. You can always learn more.
   I have found sharing my art and growing my social media has required me to learn a lot of new skills and seek to learn as much as I can. I have been reading articles and resources to learn more about social media, marketing and business. And even in improving my art skills, I watch tutorials and learn from other artists to learn how I can get better. I also learned what my audience likes and interacts with through the insights on my social media pages to gauge what type of videos I should post and the demographic that are watching my videos.

Exploring my passion for art and creativity has sparked a new level of fulfilment in my life. I find that it gives me a wonderful place to explore what I love and express myself through art. I have always enjoyed giving gifts or cards to my friends and family because I loved making something personal and one-of-a-kind for those I love. And now I am enjoying doing that for others as well!

My now husband took me to a pottery wheel-throwing class for my birthday, and that was our first time ever doing something like that! I loved the process so much and was fascinated with the concept of this art form. We picked up our pieces a few weeks later, and I was in love. We have ceramics displayed in our home, and I couldn't wait to make more. Later on, I saw a clay kit in a video I was watching online, and I bought one because I thought it would be perfect for a date night with my husband. I had so much fun and enjoyed physically creating something with my own hands that I decided to keep buying more clay and seeing what would come from it!

I feel a deeper connection with God now that I have explored working with clay. I love this beautiful verse that describes God as the potter, and we are the clay: "Yet you, Lord, are our Father. We are the clay; you are the potter; we are all the work of your hand." (Isaiah 64:8) I feel as though my passion for creating clay pieces is my desire to connect with God more.

It has also been beautiful discovering more about the character of God because we are His masterpieces. He is the true creator and artist that brings things to life. I have always been fascinated with God's creation, and my art is becoming a way to keep memories and have artwork or pieces to remember them by.

I want to be able to share my story with others and to know that God restores and has changed my life, and He can do the same with you! My best piece of advice is to believe in the gifts that God has given you and that you are intentionally created by Him for a specific purpose.

What is God calling you to? What are your gifts and talents? And how can you use them?

by   *mei*

Artist, Melanie Meihua Peeauake "By Mei"

Ceramic Pieces: *Rice Bowl, Mug, Fleur Vase & Ballerina Bowl*

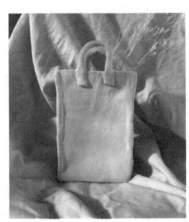

Ceramic Piece: *Tote Vase*

"Tea or Coffee"

About The Author

Melanie Meihua Peeauake is an Australian Mixed Media Artist based in Sydney. She specialises in ceramics, textured painting, and oil pastel artworks. Throughout her life, she has been fascinated with the beauty of creation. Her work focuses on God, florals, landscapes, love, and things that bring her joy. Her mission is to share my love of art, things that bring me happiness and love of God through my pieces and to bring joy and inspiration to those that receive them.

She draws inspiration from the character of God and the world around her, and her artworks provide a reminder of His provision and faithfulness.

Melanie is also passionate about creating sculptures and everyday homewares and adding her own flare with interesting shapes and designs.

FIND ME:

Facebook: by mei (https://www.facebook.com/byy.mei/)
Instagram: @by_____mei
Tiktok: @by_____mei
Email: bymei.artist@gmail.com
Website: bymeiboutique.etsy.com

The Artist Haven

Seeking God through my creativity brought me a great sense of satisfaction and joy, but it wasn't always that way. I had to give myself permission to let go of my past and step into my creative identity. Donna knows this as well. Her story talks about how to unwrap your creative gifts and talents, even when it would be easier to hide them in a box.

Dedication

I dedicate this chapter to my Lord Jesus Christ who has made me an overcomer in every way. "Commit your works to the Lord [submit and trust them to Him], And your plans will succeed [if you respond to His will and guidance]." Proverbs 16:3 (AMP)

Donna Faye

Permission To Do You

Donna Faye
Multi-Passionate Entrepreneur

Philippines

"All you've ever needed and wanted is all you've ever been.
Give yourself permission to be you."
~Stephen De Sede[29]

As a child, I had so many interests and passions that I wanted to pursue, from being a teacher to an astronaut, from doing ballet to playing the guitar and piano. I joined school clubs and church presentations to find my voice and express who I truly was.

However, as I grew older, I found myself trying to fit in with what was popular and lost sight of my true identity, masking my personality and attitude.

As life went on, I found myself getting more and more fed up with everything. It seemed like everyone else had it so easy and here I was, just struggling to fit in. I wasn't into drugs or partying like some of my peers, but I still felt like I didn't quite belong.

Growing up, I always felt like the odd one out. My hair was short and I was as thin as a rail. While my friends chattered endlessly about their latest crushes, I just couldn't seem to get

[29] DeSede, S. (n.d.) Thought leader quote. Retrieved from:
https://www.humanexp.au/human-experience-by-stephen-de-sede-4intellects

into it. It made me wonder if there was something wrong with me; if I wasn't quite human like everyone else.

The truth is, I've always had a unique way of doing things. While my mom, my classmates, and my friends all followed the same path, I always seemed to be off on my own tangent. It was like I was a puzzle piece that just didn't fit with the rest of them.

Guess what I turned to for comfort?

Food, soft drinks, and Disney shows and songs. They were my escape from reality, my way of feeling like I wasn't alone. And who knows, maybe someday I'll find my true calling, my place in this world where I fit perfectly. Until then, I'll keep dancing to my own beat and enjoying the simple pleasures that make life worth living.

The 180-degree Turn

By the age of 12, I felt there was a void that food and Disney shows can't fill. When I reached the age of 14, we had a lesson in school about values and purpose. The teacher explained it on a surface and academic level, and when I was walking home by the sunset, I asked myself: *What am I really here for? What am I living for? Am I just going to go to school every day and just simply exist?*

Voila! God was hearing me! Opportunities popped up to be able to know what I am living for through youth conferences and becoming a kids' church teacher.

Ultimately I know who I am. My identity is not in my talent, my beautiful voice, houses that we own, prestigious school that I've enrolled in nor cute face. I don't need to mask my authentic self and get in the box of what the world says I should be and what I should not be.

I no longer need to do things to be socially accepted.

I realised that my identity is in Christ Jesus; that I am who He says I am.

I am loved.

I am accepted.

I am forgiven.

When I ask what my purpose is... I thought I was only here for ONE purpose. I thought I was only called to do ONE THING. Little did I know that our purpose is different in every season.

My Journey

During my childhood years, I masked my identity and because of that I didn't really know who I was. But my journey to living authentically as a multi-passionate individual started with my acceptance.

Acceptance that I am wired differently.

I am not like my Mum who is very objective.

I am not like my Spiritual Mum, Kate, who is so focused on what she wants.

I am not like my college friends who pursued a job with only one role - their job title.

Before I came to a state of acceptance, I had a whirlwind of emotions that made me ask myself, *Why on earth I'm not like them? Why on earth can't I just be like my friends who can sit still in an office cubicle from 7 am to 5pm?*

I've had tons of questions... and I felt that my potential was going to waste. Or was it because of not being obedient? May I have missed my blessing?

But I had to ACCEPT that everybody is not the same and wired very differently.

Once I accepted myself then took a step of believing God has planted me in every season right where He wants me to be. In the sense of believing God has a plan and a future for me, I was able to take a step in pursuing what I love.

Ever since high school, I wrote songs, my classmates & I even sang in classes, and it's just amazing to feel that people are singing it because the song I've created lifts their spirit. It feels fulfilling.

Right after graduating from college, I wrote more and more songs. I have heaps of written songs in notebooks. However, when I tried to produce a song on my own, I felt like I had a hard time writing a song with a piano. I have lyrics in place and the rhythm but why on earth did I feel like I was going against the flow? I gave up. Kept all those notebooks.

Sooo, you might be wondering, what happened with the songwriting journey? Fast forward to December 2021. I was able to launch a single! The ones that have listened to it, told me that it helped them with what they're journeying through.

Soooo, you might be asking... How were you able to launch it given that you're not excellent in piano? I delegated. Eventually, one day I encountered an agency that was looking for writers.

So my online journey started. I first became an SEO Writer for various blogs and online publications, writing over 2500 words per day. It was really hard but I managed to push through given that I told myself, I loved writing songs but I can monetise it in another way, by using my gift to pay my bills. I went from song writing to SEO writing; not that far still a writer.

Slowly, many doors of opportunity came knocking on my door, I managed our family business of Real Estate Leasing, I became a Financial Advisor doing sales, connecting with people and you know what, I loved connecting with people (not entirely the quota we had to produce! Ha Ha!)

And as I am journeying through, I remembered the reason why I wanted to write songs: so that I can help people. Well, as a Financial Advisor I do help people secure their lives when an unexpected crisis happens to them.

And ultimately, I got tired of being "ghosted" by potential clients, I just stuck with doing Digital Marketing and lo and behold, my creativity that I never knew existed just popped up. Doing SEO Writing had gotten my writing ability inside the box because I had to adhere with keyword count, factual data, recent world news and keywords.

When I started creating graphics, I didn't think I was a pro because I am a Communication Arts graduate. I have classmates who are really better than me.

I thought I was dumb in creating graphics but WOW! When I did graphics, it just flowed. I didn't realise that the graphics and websites created for others were designed by me.

Eventually my confidence grew and I trusted what God has orchestrated and revealed to me. As I grew into confidence, knowing my capabilities and what I can do, the graphics and websites I designed have tripled the earnings of my clients.

It's the creative outpour from above that enabled me to design graphics and websites quickly and was a massive tool in my clients' business launching through more sign-ups and conversions. I continue creating graphics, designing websites and editing videos for clients because I love creating and being able to help build a positive world through my work.

Another dream of mine came true when prestigious universities in the Philippines hired me as their voice-over for their projects and advertisements. The videos & voice overs were featured in the Regional News Network and reached internationally.

The journey from being an SEO writer, down to doing digital marketing, designing graphics and creating websites, led me to realising I can't do it all. Yes, I can do lots of things; but I got to a point where I had to understand if I wanted to pursue things, I have to accept that "I need to delegate and trust that others are able to deliver." I need to stay in my lane with all my various skills, talents and gifts and trust that God will bring someone to my doorstep to be able to help me in achieving His plans and purposes for me in this world.

It's a whole learning journey of ABC:

Accepting

Believing

Confidence in God to grow with Him and in Him

Next Train Station

If you're like me and you feel like you don't fit in or people expect you to be "this and that" but you haven't met their expectations, all you gotta do is:

Accept

Accept where you are. Accept that God has placed you right where He wants you to be. Accept your flaws, your weaknesses but also accept the things that make you, YOU.

What is your uniqueness?

What do you love to do?

What are you excited to do?

What things make you fulfilled?

Believe that God has You in His hand

You are in the palm of God's hand and He has a great future for you. There are times that we doubt ourselves over the past mistakes that we have made and have us thinking, "Do I still deserve my calling? Do I still deserve the blessing?"

Of course, you still do! It says in Jeremiah 1:5, "Before I formed you in the womb I knew you, before you were born I set you apart."

You think God is surprised with what you did? Of course not, He is God. And that's the reason why He gave us Jesus. With Jesus, we are made whole, accepted, forgiven, loved. Believe that where you are right now is instrumental to your journey after you alight on the next station.

I'm a sucker for trains, I love riding trains and just like when a train passes through a dark tunnel, it is kinda scary. Like, what if the train stops on the middle of the tracks? Just like when we're inside the dark tunnel, there are many what ifs in life, too...

We have to grow IN Confidence in the One who has created us and called us.

Growing in Confidence

We have to put our confidence in God and from Him flows our self-confidence because if we put our confidence on only ourselves, we're only human, and we have lots of thoughts that cause us to let ourselves down. Knowing who we are in Christ makes us empowered.

What is our identity? We are a masterpiece, treasured, loved, forgiven, free, unfinished and overcomers.

"If you can do more than one thing, do YOU."

Donna Faye

Multi-passionate Entrepreneur
Thedonnafaye.com

https://genius.com/Donna-faye-fight-or-flight-lyrics

Chorus:
You put me in a fight or flight
Terrible I know
I can't control
What's going in on my head
Like Rushing
Or Crushing
Falling
Or Breaking
You get on overdrive
You put me in a fight or flight
Fight or flight
Fight or flight
Verse 1:
The thing about courage
You're burned out all the time
The thing about resilience
You push all your life

Refrain:
But
This time
I can't
Hit the wall
Breaking down oh
I think I need a crash cart
You got me on a tough spot

(Chorus)

Verse 2:
When's it gonna change
You got me feeling high
When you think you're silenced
You speak from your heart

(Refrain)
(Chorus)
You might also like
You put me in a fight or flight
Fight or flight
Fight or flight
You put me in a fight or flight
Fight or flight
Fight or flight

You can listen here:
Apple Music https://music.apple.com/lv/album/fight-or-flight-single/1599719294
Spotify
https://open.spotify.com/artist/7mykHFNZwzvbOH58usTYAq

About the Author

Donna Faye is a Multi-Passionate Entrepreneur. She runs multiple businesses which includes being a Hybrid Virtual Assistant and Digital Business Manager. Donna is a voice-over artist and in her free time, she is also a songwriter.

From piecing out strategies, streamlining business processes to creating eye-catching videos & riveting website design to convert your target audience, she is the unicorn that'll help light up the dark path you're stuck in right now.

FIND ME:
Website: https://thedonnafaye.com/

The Artist Haven

God is so gracious to reveal Himself in different ways. He gives us our confidence, our worth and shows us our value and how much we truly matter to Him. It's the love that He shows us that helps us to keep going. For me, it's been about understanding my identity in Christ. For my fellow author, Hana, this was a truth that she not only received through His word, but through a powerful vision that set her creative purpose in motion.

Dedication

First, in gratitude to God, a fountain of Wisdom and the Source of Love in my life.

Then to all those who long to be unconditionally loved. While painting the picture of the Well, I felt invited to pray for you all who are now reading this priceless testimony.

Special thanks to a precious lady, Aileen Murphy RLR, who accompanied me in love along my Irish retreat life-changing journey to the Well.

~Hana

A Life Changing Encounter At the Well

Hana Kalna
Certified Art Therapist & Bibliodramatist,
Healing Arts Coach & Mentor

Ceske Budejovice, Czech Republic

"When we long for life without difficulties, remind us that oaks grow strong in contrary winds and diamonds are made under pressure." ~ *Peter Marshall*[30]

There is a popular saying: **"An oyster that was not injured, will never produce pearls, because the pearl is a healed wound."** Yes, there are treasures in pain. When I look back at the winding path of my life so far, the painful moments unleashed the most significant growth.

I can still recall that cute, shy, really sensitive little girl with a ponytail tied up in a colored ribbon who so often felt lonely and vulnerable, trying to please those around her to earn love. I grew up as the youngest of three children. With time, I found that my easily exploited sensitivity ended up becoming one of my greatest assets, tested throughout my life. Thankfully, no circumstance got out of hand. God stepped in with His powerful protection by sending me angels with flesh and bones to assure me that He was always by my side. It was these people,

---

[30] BrainyQuote. (2023). Peter Marshall Quotes. Retrieved from:
https://www.brainyquote.com/quotes/peter_marshall_392737

circumstances, and adversities in my life that were the catalysts for my growth. I was only eight years old when I encountered the biggest love of my life, Jesus, and I received Him as my Lord and Savior.

I remember well the significant transformation of my heart that I underwent as a teenager. Despite my shame and fragility, I must say that - by the grace of God - I became a youth leader and a social interconnector. I felt like a fish in water when organizing social events and was happy on the go. Soon Jesus served as the best model for my growth and led to my decision to live a life with Christ and for his people in the world.

These days I am part of a beautiful worldwide Christian family and a local network of people with whom I share deep bonds. I have an awesome backup of close friends and lovely extended family. Moreover, I am exceptionally blessed by the call to spiritual motherhood which is proving very fruitful. I am still aware of my fragility and deep sensitivity but these have - amazingly - become additional assets to the power of the Holy Spirit, both in my leadership ministry and my healing prayer ministry where I have witnessed many of Jesus' healings. People who had suffered from psychosomatic illnesses were made whole, those who had lacked freedom, gained it through forgiveness, and I have witnessed many deep emotional wounds healed. Seeing how powerful God is, led me to study art therapy to gain more knowledge and experience in counseling and arts to reach out to all those who look for deep emotional healing and unleashing their creative potential.

Engaging in expressive arts prayerfully helps us listen to the depths of what is stirring within. I treasure the road so far traveled as priceless with the wisdom gained through the trials, so even if I could change my past, I would resist the temptation to do so. There lies a great freedom in accepting reality. My passion is equipping people to shine in their uniqueness by unlocking their hidden potential and unleashing their gifts for this world. When I went through the inner healing process years ago, I lacked this complexity of approach. The grace of being healed led me up to take art therapy to the next level. Seeing my clients who wish to unlock their best potential with me and those being broken, jagged shards transformed into bright shining diamonds is a joy.

Invited to a Life-changing Inner Journey
In May 2022 I decided to enjoy the special time of a 30-day retreat. I spent the daily, disarming silence and solitude with the Bible in hand apart from daily one-on-one meetings with my spiritual director and a worship time with the other retreatants. When listening to the voice of God, I witnessed a profoundly deep freeing transformation happening at all the levels of my whole life. I let God embrace my inner self through the power of His Word, colors and dance. Step by step, my true self started to shine like a diamond.

One day of the retreat, I found myself sitting at the well of my life in the desert, gazing into the depths at the reflection of my sad face, smelling the damp air, longing to be loved. How often had I struggled in the midst of life's adversities, questioning what kind of value I actually had at a really deep level. It was the moment I found myself as if thrown into Joseph's well. In the encounter with Joseph of Egypt I was stripped of the clothes of my false self, just like Jesus was stripped of his clothes and put on the cross for our salvation. As Christ descended into the well of my life and drew me out of the depths of the well, that place of despair became the place of Promise and Resurrection for me. Jesus then gave me a new garment: the Dignity of the beloved Daughter of God. And I was given a new name (according to Rev 2:17) as I heard God call me Tabitha, as promising to me raise to life.

I felt in my gut that I had started a significant inner transformative journey. I can still hear Jesus' invitation, *"Whoever drinks the water I give him will never thirst"* (John 4:14). Still now I can feel the cooling taste of water, quenching my existential thirst. While praying over Jesus' encounter with the Samaritan woman, I accepted the invitation to get my thirst for love quenched by Christ, the Living Water. In His *"Will you give me a drink?"* I realized the stark truth: I didn't really have anything to offer Him, but suddenly I heard His voice deep down in my heart: *"I thirst for you"*. And just when healing warmth spread through my body, I understood that the Samaritan woman's shadow had isolated her. Like in her case, Jesus allowed my wound to gently come out into the light. So I jumped in with both feet, revealed to Him all my remaining suppressed pain, stored in my subconsciousness, and said *YES* to the healing to be made whole.

A Crown Made a Well, the Fountain of Living Water

"If you knew the gift of God and who it is that asks you for a drink, you would have asked him and he would have given you living water." (John 4:10 NIV) I heard Jesus say to me.

I was invited to take a sheet of sturdy paper and put a lot of water on it. I suddenly sensed the water as sacred, meaning more than the substance, as a symbol of a new life and cleansing. A powerful surge of God's grace flooded every cell of my body and I saw myself as good enough because we deserve God's unconditional Love. How many times have we learned this fundamental truth of our worth, but have been deceived yet again?

Suddenly, I felt that I shouldn't use a paintbrush: the distance it produced between myself and the paper would not reflect the beauty of intimacy with my true self. I grasped a bottle of acrylic vermilion color for the shade of red representing blood to express the pain in my life. In the unfolding dialog with Jesus, I expressed in utter safety all my broken thoughts; when I was rejected, abandoned, and misunderstood and as a result when I had been trying hard to live up to someone else's expectations since I perceived myself as ´not good enough´. When I noticed that still present pain, I perceived that it was a Crown I had to express; Christ´s Crown of suffering. Suddenly, the red paint I spread onto the paper was the blood of my salvation whereby Jesus takes all the pain of my life onto Himself.

As I was led by the Holy Spirit to continue with that most primal form of finger painting, I felt the loving presence of God deep inside inviting me to an inner dance of making me whole. I was filled with peace and consolation and I felt profoundly connected to my entire being within. Every cell in my body was filled with warm embracing love, renewed. My deep, sedimented layers of self-doubt and shame were peeled back.

What I felt during the prayer goes far beyond words. It is better expressed and seen in my painting, which shows the flow of my finger strokes and how precisely I was led to put another foundational paint layer on the same warm red. It was the white of the present Resurrection, of healing water in the Crown and the Well. I bathed in the loving gaze of God, in the Well full of living water, with sheer joy. I was all ears to hear Jesus and sensed that the Wisdom lying within the Well held the promise that I wouldn´t thirst anymore. As soon as I gained momentum, I felt an exceeding desire to share this powerful experience with all those who thirst for unconditional love.

Then I was led to fill the Well with white ripples representing life-giving, cleansing water. I felt the salvatory power in the finger strokes of shining white, the healing torrents from Jesus' side when dying on the cross, blending with the underlying layer of red. I was powerfully driven to make two torrents of Jesus' pierced side from which gushed blood and water. I sensed Jesus' healing, cleansing power and the gift of salvation along with His everlasting presence flowing from His heart while still finger painting.

In John 19:34 we read, *"One of the soldiers pierced Jesus' side with a spear, bringing a sudden flow of blood and water."* (NIV) Yes, that was it. This was the same Jesus who poured Living water onto me and for me, Hana, who stepped into the Samaritan woman´s shoes.

Through my fingers, in the strokes dipped into shining white, I received the power of the Holy Spirit, fountain-like. I was newly anointed by the Holy Spirit and given a passion to serve others through these places, brought to life in me, with the

Living Water from John 7:37: *"Let anyone who is thirsty, come to me and drink."* (NIV)

My spontaneous dance reflected momentum. I overflowed with joy and praised the Lord for that uplifting gushing fountain as a symbol of the waters of eternal life. The fact no one was around was a sheer grace, otherwise, they would doubtless have thought me mad 😊 in the midst of that most life-giving process!

I recognized again the crown in the image of the well, but now it was the Crown of glory, inviting me to unite with Jesus in a most beautiful intimacy. Through pure white strokes, mixing up with the transformative red, I felt that I was being sent out to share this testimony with others. I had been touched by Jesus' grace many times before in my life, but now a profoundly significant transformation happened.

"You will be a crown of splendor in the Lord's hand, a royal diadem in the hand of your God." (Isaiah 62:3 NIV)

I would like to offer you Five Keys for Growth which personally helped me:

Growth Key 1: Accept Pain to Unlock your Voice
A real change deep in me started unleashing as soon as I decided to be authentic with myself. Like that I embraced the experienced pain which had triggered my mind to see reality differently. So I recommend you to open up all your senses for a deep reflective prayer to unlock your powerful Voice.

Growth Key 2: A Real Transformation is Unleashed through the Suppressed Emotions
I can witness to the fact that art therapy techniques can very effectively release emotional pain. For me, the repressed anger changed into creativity and confidence. As an art therapist, I use the techniques to ingeniously prevent common daily life problems from growing into mental health issues such as serious states of being overwhelmed, distressed, frustrated, dealing with shame, low self-worth and burnout.

Growth Key 3: Integrate your Shadow to Make a Roadway to Achieving Wholeness
In my therapeutical work, I like taking inspiration from psychiatrist and psychoanalyst C. G. Jung. For him, the Shadow was an important archetype. As you know, I viewed it as inappropriate to express my anger; my personal Shadow, in which lay a great hidden potential. This is exemplary in the Samaritan woman. She was ashamed of the repressed part of her, but when she encounters Jesus in the full light of the midday sun, which doesn't cast any shadow. She is healed; made whole.

Growth Key 4: Receive Freedom by Embracing the Self
The Self is the archetype of wholeness and self-transcendence. This is the Self that emerges after integrating our feminine and masculine aspects. And the well, central to the story, is biblically typical for integrating these aspects as a meeting place and a symbol of a new birth. For me, the received freedom at the Well feels like a refreshing gasp of wind, allowing me to be fully myself.

192

Growth Key 5: Open up to Creativity and Be Loved to Love
I have received a precious life full of wisdom: the art of reading each person's unique life story in a reverted way. In our wounds lies a truly powerful potential. This was another time God showed me in a mighty way He loves me first and with the received love I am sent to love others. Like that I praise the Lord: "You anoint my head with oil; my cup overflows" (Psalm 23:5 NIV).

I suggest these action steps:

1. Sense your body. Notice your feelings and involve all the senses on both the body and mind levels. A proper walk can help you get in touch with your body. Remember to breathe in and out deeply. If possible, take a swim in bracing sea waves.

2. Be bold. Letting God lead you out to the well may be challenging. Facing your remaining sediments of the false self is an excellent premise for a healthy transformation. The consequent unleashing of your true self doesn't happen while sitting on your hands. When facing difficult times in life, it can help you to take time out to reassess your thoughts. Lay aside your fear and doubts and move in the opposite spirit to fear.

3. Trust the process. Don't be afraid to expose your wounds and unfulfilled expectations before Him. God thirsts for you because He knows your thirst for love. Despite innate instinct to hide our wounds, God's grace reaches the most vulnerable part of ourselves.

What is your next step to take?

Listen to God's heartbeat for you

With joy, I can draw water from the Well of salvation. I have learned great wisdom, which I have the privilege to share with you here. Cherish your wounds as they are the place of your flourishing and blessings. Therein lies the potential to revert all seemingly dark or inevitable pain into a life-giving Well. There's real hope nestled in every circumstance of our life; just look at the seemingly withered Resurrection plant, which gives the beautiful, unexpected blossoms in the midst of the desert.

I have come to realise that whenever I feel the most cut-up, a diamond is taking shape - through a process of cutting, polishing and shaping to perfect symmetry in order for the diamond to reflect the maximum amount of white light. To re-discover dignity, it is worth undergoing the growing pain. For this reason, I am most grateful for those in my life who caused the biggest challenges to me.

How many times did I beat around the bush instead of bringing the pains and sorrows right away to the gentle wound Healer? I can't say I am completely healed now, or perfectly whole. There is a lingering fragility which reminds me of the need to let God go on with His loving presence and to keep working on my ongoing transformation. His love holds me! A decision to follow Him entails a lot of courage and discipline as *"Everyone who enters an athletic contest goes into strict training. They do it to win a temporary crown, but we do it to win one that will be permanent."* (1 Cor 9:25 NIV)

Receiving the permanent Crown of glory is worth any cost! In my recent vision from the Lord, I saw the heart of God was pumping, for each of us out of love! Listen to God's heartbeat for you! The gift of my inner journey is to be shared. May God bless you who reads this.

"It is precisely in cherishing our wounded places that we have the potential to reach the most flourishing and fruitful stage in our life"

Hana Kalna

"Grace Filled at the Well of My Life"
This picture captures the powerful beauty of the deep transformation I encountered. Jesus meets my deepest desires with His living water at the well of my life (John 4:1-42)

About the Author

Hana is a certified art therapist with 15 years of experience, a healing arts mentor, a Bibliodramatist and a Kingdom wholeness coach. Originally a special needs teacher and a book translator from English into Czech. She also studied theology and biblical studies and has been involved in leadership and healing ministry for about three decades. Her passion is healing art therapy business and ministry which she has launched online worldwide.

Hana has gained rich experience in using expressive arts to enhance emotional, creative and spiritual growth through art therapy techniques. She feels enthusiastic about implementing creative biblical approach of Bibliodrama into her sessions that helps people find their voice. She is the founder of Life In Abundance Academy, and Prophetic Art and Healing Facebook group. Hana loves facilitating people's deep personal transformations at psychological and spiritual levels by unleashing their true selves while accompanying them on their unique life paths. Hana cherishes reading each person's life story in a reverted way as she feels being led to recognize the rich potential in people's seemingly desolate places and just there to unlock their specific calling for this world.

FIND ME:
Website: www.hanakalna.com
Facebook: https://www.facebook.com/hana17.sarah

The Artist Haven

In my encounter with God, I saw myself and my Creator in a new way. When I was down on myself and felt hopeless, He was there. He's always there. God's promises are there for us to hold onto. We need these promises in the mountains and the valleys of our lives; when we deal with major pain and grief. LaTrina is no stranger to experiencing grief and clinging to God's goodness during tough times. As she shares in the following chapter, not only does God make beauty from ashes, but He also makes beauty from stress.

Dedication

I dedicate this chapter to my Savior & LORD, Jesus Christ, who brought me out of darkness into His marvelous light and continues to amaze me with His Love. To my gift and husband, Earl III, who constantly loves, supports, and challenges me to pursue God's call on my life. To my angel babies: Kimani, Jeremiah & Laila, who motivate me to move with purpose and say their names with grace and esteem. To my family & special friends – I love you!
~LaTrina

There _IS_ Beauty in Stress

LaTrina Bray
Infertility Advocate,
Empowerment Coach

Ohio, United States

"... Look at the lilies of the field and how they grow. They do not work or make their clothing, yet Solomon in all his glory was not dressed as beautifully as they are."
Matthew 6:28-29 NLT

I never thought I would find beauty in stress. But I do. Honestly, putting these words in a sentence and having the nerve to verbalize my statement, makes me think it sounds more like an expression of classic irony than an assertion. Right? I can imagine as one reads the title, the thought may occur, "Is she *crazy?*" No, I am not. But seriously, who am I to audaciously announce "there is beauty in stress," and intentionally seek out *beauty* as I sink bitterly into the depths of stress-filled life situations? Who am I to search for *beauty* while walking in the valley of decision? And who am I to arise from the valley, with this "mountain-top" idea, making a proclamation with a straight face and full of moxie?

Why am I looking for beauty... shouldn't I seek answers? Solutions? Hope? Well, I found them all! When considering the wisdom and confidence I gained from living it genuinely, I better understand my authority to make this powerful declaration. I invite you to journey with me and witness the beauty in stress.

Who's that Girl?

I am the eldest granddaughter on both sides of my family and have always loved babies. As a little girl playing with dolls, I innocently and instinctively knew I wanted a baby. My family always referred to me as an "old soul" and somehow, as a teenager, I was the "designated babysitter" to my younger cousins. Even my desire to be married and have a family was confirmed as I matured. If someone simply announced a pregnancy or baby shower, I hurried to the store looking for the cutest gift I could afford. To put it mildly, I loved all things 'baby': Baby clothes, baby showers, baby cuddles – everything – except the dirty baby diapers. Whew!

I imagined finding out *"I'm pregnant"* and sharing the news with my husband and family. I dreamed of experiencing my little one growing inside me. I expectantly awaited my turn to eat multiple weird food combinations, without judgment from onlookers, because I was "eating for two." I anticipated the pain of the labor and delivery – followed by immense joy and love – once I saw that angelic face staring up at me. Bathing and dressing my baby in adorable clothes, taking family pictures, celebrating holidays, and most of all, hearing my child call me *"Mama."*

Stressed... Who Me?

But my beautiful dream became a nightmare with a recurring theme, starting in February 2005 when I went to my three-month check-up. Shortly after the examination and ultrasound began, I heard the words, *"There is no heartbeat."* My heart sank. As I panicked, the doctor felt my swollen belly while trying to hide a look of concern, unconvincingly. The nurse instructed me to leave the OB/Gyn office and travel to a radiology office for a vaginal ultrasound.

Alone I sat, waiting in my car, crying uncontrollably and praying it was just a mistake – a misread ultrasound. Then I was told, matter-of-factly, the original verdict was accurate. My baby died. No reason was given. There was no comfort extended. I had plenty of questions, but no answers. And this all happened shortly after attending the funeral of my beloved, Uncle Charles. Not to mention, I was a single woman feeling the anguish of grief, as well as carrying the guilty act leading to my heartache. *Stressed*... absolutely I was.

I had endured horrendous periods for a week every month from the onset. But after I met and married my husband Earl III, in 2008, we consulted with the gynecologist and a fertility specialist for insight on our situation and starting a family. Later that same year, I persevered through recurrent ER visits, physical pain (and recovery) from surgery to remove large fibroids from my uterus, subsequent unbearable periods, as well as the monthly rollercoaster of hoping for a positive pregnancy test, only to see another negative result.

I cried daily, full of heartache, disappointment, even jealousy, as other women walked around with baby bumps and tales of their 1st, 2nd, and 3rd trimester woes. Finally, I experienced absolute joy: a "+" sign on my pregnancy test in early January 2011 – followed consequently by a phone call voicing "your HCG levels started dropping" in mid-February 2011 (shortly before my Uncle James' death). Then I got pregnant a third time and had nearly the same conversation in May 2011 for Mother's Day. Two more babies, lost. My joy stripped away again – followed by yet another surgery finalizing my journey in winter 2013.

These things were happening to me personally, but life continued. The sun still rose and set. Women were still getting pregnant and having healthy babies...why *not* me? Adding insult to injury, I had changed careers and started a new job, where one of the first questions was, "Do you have any children?" The first time someone asked me that I broke down in tears. Sometimes I ignored the question. Other times I skillfully changed the subject. Talk about stress overload!

Let's Talk About Stress
Since stress is explained differently by multiple sources, I'd like to first define what stress is. Webster's Dictionary gives one definition as, *"mental, emotional, or physical tension, strain, or distress"*; while the World Health Organization states, *"Stress can be defined as a state of worry or mental tension caused by a difficult situation. Stress is a natural human response that prompts us to address challenges and threats in our lives. Everyone experiences stress to some degree. The way we respond to stress, however, makes a big difference to our overall well-being[31]."* Over the years, I can't even recall how many times I have heard the phrase, "Stress *can* kill you!" whether uttered casually as a joke, or a warning from my parents.

---

[31] World Health Organization. "Stress." Retrieved from: *who.int/news-room/questions-and-answers/item/stress*, February 21, 2023.

But, true? Nah, couldn't be — even though I was experiencing tremendous stress, I refused to admit the reality of "feeling like I was dying" to myself or anyone else at that time. I agree that *"everyone experiences stress to some degree"* and this stress was major and constant. I've had stress triggered from financial to employment issues, relationships, and death. But the most painful, persistent stress came after I suffered the loss of my babies: Kimani, Jeremiah, and Laila and from not having *any* living children. I've been warned of how stress affects people: physically, mentally, emotionally (let me add socially, spiritually, and economically too). There were occasions when I was so stressed, I gained weight from "stress eating" and times I lost weight from being *too* stressed to eat. I have cut my hair because it was shedding too much, experienced insomnia for weeks, cried so exhaustively I felt dehydrated, been so angry I wanted to hit something terribly hard *(like Sally Field in Steel Magnolias)*. I've also been so mad at God that I refused to pray.

Bridge Over Troubled Water
Consequently, I read recommendations on ways to alleviate stress, including modifying my diet, exercising, meditation, getting more sleep, and laughing more. *Laughing* more? Oh yes, I did laugh heartily and sarcastically, *after* I rolled my eyes in disbelief at its simplicity. Now, during these difficult years, my husband consistently bought me flowers. Once they wilted, I disposed of the flowers and reused the vases.

One day, I desired to beautify our new home and began making floral arrangements, using faux flowers and colourful stones, came to my mind. I loved this idea because I adored flowers, but honestly was "sick of death." I visited three craft stores to buy necessary materials. Then I dedicated time to sit alone, in the living room, to make my creative floral idea into tangible art. I made one quickly, then another one. One arrangement I made, thinking of my daughter, Kimani, with tears streaming down my face, took seemingly forever to complete. But I did! Then I began taking my time, focusing on the smallest details of my art – stone by stone, flower by flower – thinking about everything and processing my unaddressed emotions and pain. As I listened to either gospel music or old school R&B, I had "a little talk with Jesus." After I finished, I named each arrangement to ensure its originality. I now had an outlet *and* trademark.

During the night, sometimes a title or phrase came into my heart, so I would get up and talk to the Lord. These words became poems. Just like that – I had two creative outlets to process my pain – allowing something beautiful to come from my creative expression. In prayer, I admitted to God what *really* hurt and bothered me, telling Him all about my troubles. Amazingly, something happened *in* me – my perspective started to change! My entire outlook and attitude about my circumstances started to shift. I began to *accept* my life as it was, allowing me to start moving forward. I was no longer imprisoned in "baby jail."

And I discovered how to respond differently to difficult people. For instance, I had a coworker, who initially was nice, but started acting "mean as a rattlesnake" toward me, after a simple misunderstanding. Puzzled, I tried to be personable and civil to no avail. However, every day was like torture because we worked in such proximity. I distinctly remember praying in my car, *Lord, You said to love our enemies, but this is hard. What does this look like for me?* Later that day, I was watching TV and saw a Joyce Meyer video, where she shared a difficult situation with someone and how God instructed her to give the person a gift. Aha! Truthfully, I thought, "I don't want to. She *won't* receive it! Anyway, *what* would I give her?" But instinctively, I discerned <u>that</u> was my answer. I asked my husband if I sounded like a fanatic, or a fool. He said, "if you're being obedient to God, what difference does it make!" I conceded and made the only beautiful thing I could – a floral arrangement.

Thinking positively, I made it with care and intricate detail; it had beautiful white and canary yellow roses. Satisfied, I looked at the finished product, noticing the five yellow roses. Immediately, I understood why God wanted me to make it. In scripture, the number *"five"* is symbolic for *"grace"* – exactly the name I chose. God was teaching me how to sow grace *(undeserved favor)* to someone else. When I gave her the birthday gift (initially, I refused to celebrate her birthday), she hugged me and told me it was beautiful. On my drive home, I understood that my obedience to God led to forgiveness in me – even when her "rattlesnake" behavior returned I was not bothered. I let go of the hurt and stress; I was at peace. In this, I was a peacemaker.

> *"Blessed are the peacemakers, for they will be called children of God."* (Matthew 5:9 NIV)

What *IS* "The Beauty?"

How does my journey relate to the declaration "there IS beauty in stress"? Well, I've been depressed; so deep down in a pit of despair that I considered taking my own life. I've been so lonely, though surrounded by people, that the room seemed as empty as I felt. My heart has been so broken that I imagined it jumping out of my chest and slowly beating on the floor, as I watched it stop, then shatter into pieces. But God! Although the question remains... what *IS* the beauty in stress? The *beauty* **IS** God Himself. He **IS** the Calm in my stressful circumstances. He **IS** the Joy in my sorrow. God **IS** the Peace in my storm. He **IS** Comfort to my broken heart. He **IS** always there with me, even when I am troubled. He **IS** the Friend when I feel alone "in the midnight hour."

"I can never escape from your Spirit! I can never get away from your presence! If I go up to heaven, you are there. If I go down to the grave, you are there." (Psalm 139:7-8 NLT)

Life was confusing and I had too many questions to number. So, I asked. I sought the LORD and studied His Word *because* I needed answers. The LORD patiently guided and reminded me of His Promises, even when I did not allow myself to receive them because I reasoned the answers had to be "deeper". But the truth was simple: **GOD REALLY LOVES ME. GOD REALLY CARES ABOUT ME!**

> *"I sought the LORD, and He heard me,*
> *and delivered me from all my fears."*
> (Psalm 34:4 KJV)

Yes, the Bible tells the truth that Jesus loves me – He suffered, bled, died, rose for and cares about me – but I now _know_ it. The truth IS reality for me. I know Him intimately from personal experience. Knowing Him *changed* me! And my behavior improved because I have a creative way to handle stress and other challenges. There it is again... *beauty*! When I proactively seek and select materials to make unique floral art to bless others or use poetic words intentionally to express my emotions and reflect experiences I have endured – Beauty shines! My life is purposeful when I coach women with similar struggles or teach His Word. By choosing to use my gift of creativity, I found a practical way to see, seek, and serve God, in spite of my trials, resulting in a more intimate relationship with my God.

"Come close to God, and God will come close to you." (James 4:8 NLT)

I acknowledge the "worldly" coping alternatives I previously tried, were a "temporary fix" and failed to work for me. So, I choose to let the Holy Spirit lead me to peaceful places and accept the gift of His peace, trusting in its sufficiency. I've learned to let God **BE** God.

"He lets me rest in green meadows;
he leads me beside peaceful streams."
(Psalm 23:2 NLT)

"Peace I leave with you; my peace I give you.
I do not give to you as the world gives.
Do not let your hearts be troubled and do not be afraid."
(John 14:27 NLT)

I no longer see myself as powerless and without refuge from trouble, but as a child of Almighty God. And "giving God all my worries and concerns" is not some Christian colloquialism to spout piously – it *is* true. I *can* live it by allowing myself to honestly <u>admit</u> my feelings about a situation OR <u>admit</u> I don't have an immediate answer to my problem, OR <u>admit</u> I have NO IDEA what to do, but I am trusting in my Heavenly Father to guide and equip me. Because I am *in* relationship with the LORD, then I am empowered to deal with my stress and challenges better. He has what I seek, whether I like the answer or not. Therefore, I seek Him about what to do in each situation, then live according to His Word without seeing the result yet. Now that's *faith*... who knew?!

Nuggets of Wisdom
While stress, daily or situational, is not ideal and does not *feel* good, it can be overcome. It's possible! Do I always get it right? Nope. However, I wholeheartedly believe God has given me *(and you)* creative gifts and ability to cope with life's challenges victoriously. I humbly share the wisdom I received from experience for practical life application:

"Let the peace of Christ rule in your hearts, since as
members of one body you were called to peace.
And be thankful..." (Colossians 3:15 NIV)

1. **P**ray – I give <u>all</u> my concerns and challenges to God. I have a little talk with Jesus in my car, at work, in my war room (yes, I have a war room). Pray first, *not* last. Pray daily, *not* infrequently. Truth is – God cares. God is able and will help me. Let Him! Don't believe the enemy's lie *"this problem is too small for God"*, or *"this doesn't really matter"*. (Philippians 4:6-7; 1 Peter 5:7)

2. **E**xpress – I identify my God-given talents and creative outlets that truly calm me. Then I show my art with my husband, or a close friend. Thank God for the gifts He has given me, uniquely. Do not minimize or compare my creativity with another person. Creativity is NOT one-size-fits-all. I am unique! (Psalm 139:14; Ephesians 2:10)

3. **A**dmit – I am honest about everything stressing me – my feelings, mistakes, fears, failures and hopes...everything! Hiding my emotions never benefited me in any way. Being truthful with God helps me process, understand, and move forward. He already knows what I need and has already made provision. (Matthew 6:8; Hebrews 4:12-13)

4. **C**hoose – I willingly decide to exercise my creativity, instead of negative emotions and habits. (Psalm 25:12

5. **E**ncourage – I seek opportunities to give cheerfully to someone else. Share money or kindness...My time...A word of encouragement – it makes a difference because giving is not solely financial! Ultimately, I will be blessed by the experience. (2 Corinthians 9:7)

When I put all of this together, I will FIND what I SEEK. **P.E.A.C.E.!**

What Can I Do, LaTrina?

Friend, I do not know what you are experiencing in life or what you have endured. However, I do know in this life stress is inevitable. These are three fundamental guidelines you can do when managing your stress:

1. **Admit** when you are stressed. Don't hide it, mask it, or explain it away. Stop looking at and thinking of yourself as "weak" because you are struggling with something. You're not weak – just human.

2. **Be** a peacemaker. Seek God first; let Him be your peace. Pursue peace to find it. Once obtained, WORK to maintain it. Then share it. Situations are different for everyone, but the work required is the same. It takes work to live peaceably with all people. It takes effort to "be still" when life seems tumultuous. It requires restraint to let go of unhealthy situations or people. Living in peace is not automatic or easy. Jesus already paid for it at Calvary – you either *accept* or *reject* it, but the gift of peace is available.

3. **Choose** to express yourself creatively in your storm. Make a conscious choice to use your OWN creative outlet. God has already given you something special to help you cope...Sing. Paint. Draw. Cook. Garden. CHOOSE TO USE IT!

Stress beware! God **IS** why I declare, "There *IS* Beauty in Stress." You can too! *Will* you?

> *"And we know that in all things God works for the*
> *good of those who love Him,*
> *who have been called according to His purpose."*
> (Romans 8:28 NIV)

LaTrina Bray

Count It All Joy

Count it all joy
Please, tell me how
So many mountains and valleys
Since that day until now

Heart gripped by sorrow
Will it ever let go?
My emotions are raging
Baby shower? Uh, I think NO!

Down a deep and dark hole
My way out – will I find?
On my tear-stained pillow
Am I losing my mind?

Fall colors, Winter snow
Days shorter, longer nights
Engulfed by this darkness
Wait... I see a Light!

As I share the truth
A smile appears on my face
Now, how did that happen?
By experience...Amazing Grace

To peace from confusion and anger
Never thought I could M.E.N.D.
Pain is now purpose
Since I talked to my Friend

Joy in suffering
Not a fairytale or a dream
Just Truth plus expectation
And someday, reality

My heart beholds a reunion
With our two girls and baby boy
You see my HOPE is in Jesus
That's how I can Count it All Joy!

Written by LaTrina Bray
(Mother of Kimani, Jeremiah, and Laila)
© LaTrina Bray 7/2019

"Indigo You"

About the Author

LaTrina Bray is an up-and-coming author and poet. She has penned thought-provoking poetry on the journey of infertility, as well as a published article. LaTrina is a born-again believer and follower of Jesus Christ. LaTrina has served on the Intercessory Prayer and Sign Language ministries to name a few, but she is also a spirited voice for women struggling with infertility and loss. LaTrina has been a featured local speaker in the community, as well as on the renowned podcasts, *That Infertility Chic*, *Bridging the Gap & Passing the Baton*, and *Thriving Woman*. Likewise, LaTrina was highlighted in the 2022 Hoinser Annual Book. She is Director of the Ohio Chapter of M.E.N.D. (Mommies Enduring Neonatal Death), an inspirational advocate, as well as a zealous Empowerment Coach of a tailor-made program for infertile women.

Not only a fierce champion for women, but LaTrina has been an enthusiastic Bible Study teacher for 20 years, using effective and innovative methods for practical application. She is married to her husband, Earl III, and devoted to her family and friends. LaTrina's desire is to glorify the LORD her God, while making a powerful and meaningful impact on the lives of others.

FIND ME:
Facebook:
https://www.facebook.com/groups/barrenandboldlybeautiful
Email: bysb3lighthouse@yahoo.com
Email: unique2Udesigns@yahoo.com *(for custom floral arrangements)*

In Closing...

Upon reflection of seeing this book, *The Artist Haven,* come together with so much beauty and creativity. I found along the way many souls wanting to find a safe haven, where they too could explore and express and share their stories of courage and determination. This book gave them a safe haven to share with faith and belief in themselves and their creativity.

But in order to step into their creative expression and identity, the authors of *The Artist Haven* needed to harness their pain to use for this artistic purpose. While this type of growth is possible for all to flourish as artists and creatives, we need to first experience this transformation in our own lives, and in our own stories.

So today I invite you to continue to connect with me and my co-authors in our sequel International book, *Moving from Brokenness to Freedom,* where we will read of others transformation and be inspired to move from brokenness to freedom.

~Coach Carmel

"There is the mud, and there is the lotus that grows out of the mud. We need the mud in order to make the lotus."
~ Thich Nhat Hanh[32]

For more information: please contact Carmel at Carmel's Garden - https://www.carmelsgarden.com/

---

[32] Goodreads.com. Retrieved from:
https://www.goodreads.com/quotes/799997-there-is-the-mud-and-there-is-the-lotus

Made in the USA
Columbia, SC
18 August 2023

21746439R00117